Help!
I'm Laughing
and I Can't Get Up

Other Books by Liz Curtis Higgs

Nonfiction for women:

"One Size Fits All" and Other Fables
Only Angels Can Wing It, the Rest of Us Have to Practice
Forty Reasons Why Life Is More Fun After the Big 4–0
Mirror, Mirror on the Wall, Have I Got News for You!

Fiction for young children:

The Pumpkin Patch Parable
The Parable of the Lily
The Sunflower Parable
The Pine Tree Parable

Help!
I'm Laughing
and I Can't Get Up

Liz Curtis Higgs

A JANET THOMA BOOK

THOMAS NELSON PUBLISHERS
Nashville

Printed in the United States of America

Published in Nashville, Tennessee, by Thomas Nelson, Inc., Publishers.

The Bible version used in this publication is THE NEW KING JAMES VERSION. Copyright © 1979, 1980, 1982, 1990, Thomas Nelson, Inc., Publishers.

Portions of chapters 7, 8, 10, and 13 first appeared in *Today's Christian Woman*, a publication of CTI, Inc.

Portions of Chapter 2 first appeared in *Marriage Partnership*, a publication of CTI, Inc.

Library of Congress Cataloging-in-Publication Data

Higgs, Liz Curtis.
  Help! I'm laughing and I can't get up / Liz Curtis Higgs.
    p.   cm.
  ISBN 0-7852-7614-9 (pbk.)
    1. Christian life—Humor. 2. Higgs, Liz Curtis. I. Title.
BV4515.2.H54   1998
248.4'02'07—dc21
                                                    97-52571
                                                    CIP

Printed in the United States of America.

7 8 9 10 11 12 QPV 03 02 01 00 99

Dedication

This book is dedicated to the funniest man I have ever known—my handsome, loving, brilliant, dry-of-wit, full-of-fun, fabulous "Foggy" Bill

Table of Contents

Acknowledgments

Forewarning: Abandon Soap, All Ye Who Enter Here

Acknowledgments

Most writers are indebted to so many people by the time a book hits the store shelves that it would require yet another volume to thank them all! Forgive me if I limit myself to one heartfelt page (alright, so I needed a smidge more on a second) of gratitude to some very special people who made sure that I could stand up rather than fall down through the seemingly endless process of putting this book together:

- To more than five hundred fabulous folks from all fifty states, plus Germany, Australia, Canada, Scotland, and France, who contributed their stories and surveys—may the finished product give you half as much joy as you gave me.

- To Gloria Looney and her nimble fingers for putting hundreds of stories, facts, and funnies on disk for me, thereby giving me a fighting chance at hitting my deadline—bless you, Mrs. Looney.

- To Janet Thoma and Todd Ross, my editors and encouragers—thanks for catching my vision for this project.

- To Dennis Hill, whose own sense of humor and playfulness is captured here in delightful black and white (and red all over!)—you, sir, are a hoot.

- To Sara Fortenberry, awesome literary agent, who believes in my dreams and then supports them.

- To some twelve hundred meeting planners across these United States who have invited me to bring a dose of humor to their amazing audiences over the last dozen years—your enthusiasm for this message made every airplane meal (almost) delicious!

- To my humor buddies, on the platform and on the page, who keep me laughing—thanks for helping me practice what I preach.

- To my online LoveKnot sisters—thanks for all your prayers!

- To my precious children, Matthew and Lillian, who put up with a lot of pizza while Mom was screaming, "Help! I'm writing and I can't get up"—extra cheese and lots of hugs for both of you! XOXO

- Most of all, to you, dear reader—bless you for being wise enough to include laughter in your life. Pass it on!

Forewarning: Abandon Soap, All Ye Who Enter Here

Skip the Safeguard, toss the Ivory, give Dial the old heave-ho: This book contains nothing but clean humor!

No need to wash out your mouth with soap after you've read a passage aloud to a friend.

No smarmy innuendos to make you blush, nor four-letter words to offend (unless you count *hoot*).

No put-downs to tickle your funny bone while bruising someone else's.

Nothing but good, clean humor that fills rather than empties, lifts rather than flattens, encourages rather than disheartens.

I agree with Carma from Utah who says, "Laughing feels so good when it's clean and everyone can enjoy the laugh."

Trust me. This book is so clean it squeaks like a duck! Dive right in, my friend, the water's fine.

PART ONE

Encouraging People Through Laughter

You are holding this book for three possible reasons:

1. You enjoy laughing.
2. Someone who knows you thinks you aren't laughing enough.
3. You're visiting a friend's house, and this book was in their reading basket next to the bathtub.

Whether you chose to be here or were dragged into this, I'm thrilled to have you along for the read. Especially since this book won't be funny without you.

That's right. You, babe. All a humorist can do is provide an opportunity for laughter, but you're the one who makes the noise.

Start whenever you're ready.

Chapter 1

🐝

Your Jest
Is as Good
as Mine

I have had a "call" to literature of a low order—humorous.
It is nothing to be proud of, but it is my strongest suit.
—Mark Twain

I make a living encouraging people through laughter. For years I didn't have the nerve to call myself a humorist. Too scary. What if they didn't laugh?

But they did laugh. Even when I wasn't being funny (which was *really* scary).

Then people started making me laugh. (Laughter is, after all, contagious.) I found scribbled notes stuffed in my purse when I wasn't looking. Long, chatty letters arrived in my mailbox. When I included a humor survey with an issue of my free newsletter, *The Laughing Heart®*, more than five hundred people from all fifty states responded with their own funny experiences, many of which landed between the covers of this book.

It's easier to share humor from the platform than on paper because when I'm watching an audience live and in person, I immediately know if something is funny or not. If it's not, I stop! The apostle John said it so well:

Having many things to write to you, I did not wish to do so with paper and ink; but I hope to come to you and speak face to face, that our joy may be full. (2 John 12)

In the meantime, though, we'll share some joy with "paper and ink"!

Our laughter correspondents also offered specific feedback on how important humor is to their well-being. On a scale of 1 to 10, they collectively gave humor a solid 8.9. Susan from Oklahoma rated her need for laughter at a 10, adding that, "Laughter lifts my heart and the hearts of others nearby."

And how often are we laughing in any given twenty-four hours? According to our survey, we're averaging 8.57 big laughs a day. There were those who were off the chart with their number of daily laughs. Stacy from California says she's hitting 600 laughs a day, and Rick must be a mathematician because he clocked his at exactly 143 per day. No more, no less, no kidding.

Most of us hovered in the single digits, though, and as Sherry from Oregon put it, "When I can *count* the number of times, it hasn't been enough." Clearly there's some remedial work to be done, but aren't you clever to realize that fact and to be right here where you belong?

Fly Away Home

Linda related an incident from the years when she and her air force hubby were stationed in California. She was cleaning house one day while their bird was singing away in his cage. Efficient woman that she was, Linda thought, *I have my sweeper out, why not tidy up the birdcage?*

The vacuum proved to be too much for the little bird to resist, and in seconds he was suctioned over to the bars of the cage. Linda quickly turned off the vacuum, but it was too late. The bird jumped on his perch, chirped once, and dropped to the bottom of the cage.

The life had literally been sucked out of him, poor thing.

Bye-bye birdie.

Linda panicked and ran to the phone, called the air force base, and told them it was an emergency and to get her jet-engine technician husband off the flight pad, a major no-no in the military. Her husband ran to the phone, scared to death until she told him what had happened.

As upset as he was about the dead bird, he was more upset about what he was going to tell his commanding officer, who would demand to know what emergency was important enough to call him off the flight pad.

Linda's husband is a clever and resourceful man. He told his CO that his wife was upset because her "Aunt Birdy" had died.

Then the unexpected happened. Flowers and sympathy cards began arriving from their friends on the base. People started asking questions about funeral arrangements for poor Aunt Birdy. Linda and her husband were mortified, but couldn't retract their story or he'd get in serious trouble.

(I imagine that, in lieu of flowers, the family of the deceased requested donations be made to the Audubon Society.)

You're Joking

Like the Aunt Birdy story, almost all of the funny material I received was original stuff from someone's own life. But a few folks shared classic jokes that tickled their funny bones.

Every joke I've ever heard has three things in common:

1. It's fairly brief and to the point, without many specific details.
2. It has a predictable format of setup and punch line.
3. It flies right out of your head two minutes after you hear it.

How many times have we started to tell a joke we just heard and end up petering out halfway through? "No, wait! I think it was the duck that said . . ." People walk away from us, disgusted. The only thing worse than not understanding the punch line is not *delivering* the punch line.

Which is why I never tell jokes. Occasional one-liners, maybe, but they're my own creation so I don't have as much trouble remembering them. I spare myself a lot of social angst by never saying, "Have you heard the one about . . .?" In fact, humorists agree that true-to-life stories work best.

Jeanne Robertson, a former Miss North Carolina and the reigning queen of the humor platform, draws almost all of her humor from her own life experiences. She says, "When a female humorist tries to use those old jokes—the football coach, the traveling salesman—they just don't work." Jeanne observes that while men are happy hearing an old joke, women want to hear stories they can relate to.

Our humor survey turned up exactly the same results: When it's time to laugh, we all agreed that our best resource is personal experience. Psychologist Judith Tingley finds that women especially respond to "anecdotal, conversational stories that deal with people, feelings, and relationships rather than the topics men prefer to laugh about—business, money, and sports."

George Bernard Shaw declared, "My way of joking is to tell the truth; it's the funniest joke in the world."

Amusing truth is everywhere. Dottie from Kentucky faxed me a note that said, "I just came from the store and noticed on the stand a copy of *Prevention* magazine, which said on the cover: FLATTEN YOUR TUMMY; SIMPLIFY YOUR LIFE. Surely they meant those to be two different articles!"

(Surely they did, Dottie, because otherwise it would be a joke about losing weight, and everyone knows there is nothing funny about that . . .)

Real-life humor comes in several flavors. My humor buddy Carl Hurley, Ed.D., subscribes to the theory that every humorous story fits into one of three categories:

1. It happened exactly that way.
2. It happened almost that way.
3. It could have happened that way.

This book will be filled with all three, but here's the scary thing: Neither you nor I will know for sure which one is which. The good news is, it doesn't matter! Artistic or comedic license requires that we stay within the bounds of truth while still producing the results that everybody wants—laughter. As long as it fits our guidelines for good, clean humor, I won't sweat the details if you won't.

I get tickled when an audience participant comes up to me after a program and asks in amazement, "Did that really happen exactly like that?!?" Hmm. *Exactly* meaning "verbatim," "every jot and tittle as it happened," "every detail precisely accurate"? Well, probably not Since I create stories from weird things that happen to me, some of which occurred years ago, I may not remember my exact words at the time or the exact order of things, but something happened all right!

If you want exact truth, read the Bible. If you're willing to forego accuracy in favor of laughter, then I'm your woman. I must admit, I've wondered what would happen if I answered the did-this-really-happen question with, "No, I made the whole thing up, from beginning to end." Would people ask for their money back? Ask for their laughter back? Ask for my head on a platter?

Why not relax and enjoy the tale? Genuinely funny stories usually have their roots in the truth, because everybody knows you can't beat real life for real humor.

Judy from California shares a story about a woman who was standing in line at an ice-cream store in coastal California when Robert Redford strolled in. (Sigh.) He walked up behind her in line, and the woman decided to play it cool.

She turned, smiled, said hello, then turned back and placed her order. After she paid for her cone and went outside, she realized she didn't have her ice cream.

Robert Redford was still waiting in line when the woman went back in, got the counter girl's attention, and told her she hadn't given her the cone.

The girl answered, "Yes I did, ma'am. You put it in your purse."

Could this have happened? You bet. (Honey, I would probably have put the ice cream in my *blouse* and not noticed.)

Watered Down . . .and Across . . .and Through

Iris and Bill from Pennsylvania were moving their son's possessions from his apartment. To set the scene, Bill was a professional truck driver who'd driven all night for twelve exhausting hours. It was late August, and the temperature outside had hit ninety degrees—it was even worse in this third-floor apartment. The young man owned a queen-size water bed that took up so much space that Iris and Bill had to slosh their way across it just to reach the other side of the room.

Suddenly, the pine box that held the bladder collapsed onto the floor, dropping six hundred gallons of encased water onto their feet. They knew they'd have to drain it before they could ever hope to get it out of the apartment, but they didn't have a siphon handy.

Bill decided they could push this humongous water balloon out the bedroom door, turn a ninety-degree corner, and force it through the bathroom door to the shower, where he could simply hold the spout open and it would drain.

Sounds easy enough.

Bill grabbed onto the end of the waterbed bladder, braced his feet against the wall, and shoved a corner out the door. It slipped from his hand and slopped back, almost knocking him over.

Then he crawled over that full, cold bladder to the other side and tried again, shoving harder, while Iris sat on the floor near the door trying to compress it, hoping to make it more narrow so it would fit through the door.

Six hundred gallons do not a skinny water bed make.

Iris glanced up to see hubby's face the color of a ripe tomato, contrasted with the, uh, "blue" air around them, and she started to laugh when all at once the whole bladder sloshed back—whump!—pinning her underneath it.

Can't you see the headline now? WOMAN KILLED BY FULL BLADDER.

Her husband lifted the edge enough for her to crawl out. Then they shoved and pulled for another ninety minutes, finally forcing the bladder out the bedroom door toward the kitchen. The bladder took advantage of its sudden freedom and took off—slop, gurgle, slurp, plop—not stopping until it reached the far side of the kitchen, traveling ten feet all by itself.

By now Iris was laughing hysterically and Bill was so mad she worried about him having a heart attack. His sense of humor became nonexistent as he feverishly pushed and shoved the six-hundred-gallon body of water, which had a mind of its own. Another hour passed before they forced it across the kitchen— one slop forward, two slops back.

At last they reached the bathroom doorway. They pushed, shoved, pulled, jumped—anything to get it to move through that tiny bathroom door. No luck. Bill leaped like a frog from the kitchen onto the bladder, bounced off, rolled into the bathroom, and hit the wall. "Oh, boy! Whee!!"

All of a sudden the bladder moved. Half of it went through the bathroom door so fast and so hard that it hit the pipes under a little freestanding sink. Slopping back, it pinned Bill to the shower stall. Iris laughed so hard that she was the one leaking now.

Bill whipped out his hunting knife, grabbed that water bed like it was a wild boar, and cut the end off in one fell swoop, prepared for an explosion of water. The water barely moved. It was at best a trickle, and only if they held the cumbersome thing at the correct angle. Out came the knife again. A bigger hole. Even so, it took four hours to drain the bladder, which added up to one very long day.

Iris couldn't stop laughing, and every time she looked at her husband, she'd start anew. The bladder, meanwhile, died a slow, painful death, drop by drop, oblivious—or is that *o-blob-ious?*—of the havoc it had created.

And the laughter. Never forget the laughter.

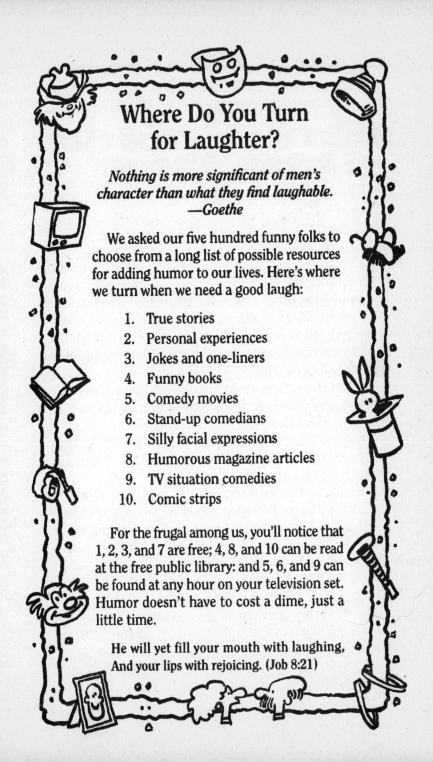

Where Do You Turn for Laughter?

Nothing is more significant of men's character than what they find laughable.
—Goethe

We asked our five hundred funny folks to choose from a long list of possible resources for adding humor to our lives. Here's where we turn when we need a good laugh:

1. True stories
2. Personal experiences
3. Jokes and one-liners
4. Funny books
5. Comedy movies
6. Stand-up comedians
7. Silly facial expressions
8. Humorous magazine articles
9. TV situation comedies
10. Comic strips

For the frugal among us, you'll notice that 1, 2, 3, and 7 are free; 4, 8, and 10 can be read at the free public library: and 5, 6, and 9 can be found at any hour on your television set. Humor doesn't have to cost a dime, just a little time.

He will yet fill your mouth with laughing, And your lips with rejoicing. (Job 8:21)

Chapter 2

Hold Your Clootie! Sheep Ahead!

A Scottish mist may wet an Englishmen to the skin.
—Thomas Fuller

My humorist buddy Jeanne Robertson says when you see something funny, don't just jot it down, write it up. A single word, even a phrase, will be meaningless in a few days, so she advises that you keep writing until you've captured the whole funny scene for posterity.

Not that I always follow this wise counsel. I have a file folder full of foolishness, tiny scraps of paper featuring stump-the-humorist phrases like, "Man in hat."

What man? What hat? Where was I when I saw this chap in his chapeau? And the most important question of all: Why was this man's hat so amusing?

I'm forced to toss such scraps in the circular file, gazing with a rather desperate longing at another piece of potentially potent humor, lost between the folds of my gray matter, never to be seen again.

My friend Evelyn, a very funny radio personality, wore a tablet around her neck to keep track of her humor sightings, which produced a few unexpected giggles of its own. Strangers who saw her in action assumed she was unable to speak and started doing mime or sign language to attempt to communicate with her. She never corrected them, of course.

The only time I have faithfully kept a careful daily humor journal was when Bill and I spent ten glorious days in Scotland for our tenth wedding anniversary. Since I was driving (on the wrong side of the road, mind you), I recorded every amusing sight on a microcassette recorder (which made me feel like the spy who came in from the cold). Then each night while it was all still fresh in my jet-lagged mind, I transferred my musings into more decipherable sentences on my laptop computer.

Driving along, microcassette in one hand, camera in the other, I was one happy lassie. Bill was certain that by the end of the ten days I'd be talking into my Kodak and trying to take pictures with my tape recorder.

Oh, ye of little faith. I did no such thing. Not only do I have pages of warm and funny remembrances, captured forever, but now all I have to do to "be there" again is to unfold my photo album, read the words on the computer screen, and it's sheep and tartans, as far as the eye can see.

Granted, I couldn't tell you what I was doing last Monday, but on Monday, May 27, 1996, I was munching on a clootie dumpling at a basement restaurant in Inverness.

Oh, Caledonia!

On paper, it sounded like heaven: Ten days in bonny Scotland, one for each year of our marriage. Just us and no kids, like a honeymoon without the jitters. We'd watched *Rob Roy*, we'd seen *Braveheart*, we were ready.

Eight hours on a plane later, we found out why they call it *jet lag*. Our bodies were in Great Britain, but the rest of us was lagging somewhere over the Atlantic Ocean. Or Greenland.

And what was our first task? Stuff our exhausted, bleary-eyed bodies into a tiny rental car, get behind the wheel on the right side of the car, and drive down the wrong side of the road. Well, wrong to us. Very right to the Scots, and in fact, the only safe option.

It was soon easy to pick out the other tourists—they were the ones using turn signals.

I was driving; Bill was navigating. Correction: I was hyper-ventilating, and Bill was working with a map the size of a table-cloth in a car no bigger than a bread box. On our honeymoon, we'd had a few minor disagreements about where to eat or when to stop for a stretch break. Now, ten years later, the stakes were much higher—we had what the Scots call an *argle-bargle* over which road would get us out of the airport, for heaven's sake.

"It's that way!" I insisted at full volume.

"Stay in the right lane! I mean, the correct lane. No, the left lane!" Bill barked back.

Peace reigned once again when we saw a sign marked WAY OUT, the first of many postings that had us doing double takes. The yield sign read GIVE WAY; a roadside trash barrel became a REFUSE TIP; and highway construction was announced with a simple ! by the road.

We were less certain about the sign that commanded LIT-TER PLEASE or the enigmatic HEAVY PLANT CROSSING, which suggested a large, leafy ficus being dragged across the pavement. Then there was the petrol station sign that warned No NAKED LIGHTS. Certainly not, even if we were married.

Businesses announced their trade with equally amusing results: A television repair place was called TELLY ON THE BLINK, an auto body repair place offered SPRAY PAINTING AND PANEL BEATING, and for those who favor self-serve shopping, one market invited you to BAG YOUR OWN MANURE, 70 PENCE A BAG. Your neighborhood pharmacist would be a DISPENSING CHEMIST, the BREAKDOWN MER-CHANT handled road service needs, and the most engaging place was the village called YETTS OF MUCKHART.

Driving along the A-75 into Dumfries, we were so taken with the pastoral scenery and the Solway Firth stretched to our south that we hardly spoke at all. On our honeymoon, we'd read aloud every sign to one another and chatted constantly, trying to take in both our surroundings and the strange and wonderful reality of marriage.

Now that our relationship was even stranger and more wonderful, we often communicated silently, holding hands. A gentle squeeze meant "I love you." A tender tap meant "Don't miss what's out the window." A soft caress meant "Only six hours until bedtime." A sudden grip meant "Don't hit the sheep!"

Indeed, sheep rule in Scotland. The edge of town wasn't marked by convenience stores and car dealerships, just sheep grazing in the fields, by the fence, on the road, under our car. Rather than branding their sheep, the Scots spray-paint them. Picture a fluorescent red design on the south end of a northbound sheep. It looked like sheep vandalism.

The little wee ones with their sweet black faces and wobbly knees fairly bleated to the animal lover in me, "Pick me up. Take me home. Baaa." Of course, we couldn't really do that—Delta Air Lines has laws about such cargo—but I considered briefly the merits of a temporary kidnapping.

Perhaps we could keep the baby sheep with us as a backseat pet. Find him a bottle of milk at the naked lights place, maybe. Eventually we'd have to put the little beastie back where we found him, though, and chances are excellent that the mother sheep wouldn't look kindly on this arrangement at all.

When I shared this wooly fantasy with Bill, he assured me we'd have to remain sheepless in Scotia.

We also saw signs posted near farms advertising FREE RANGE CHICKENS, which made us wonder if they laid free range eggs that customers gathered in u-pick-it fashion.

Oddly, neither lamb nor chicken appeared on most Caledonia menus. Haggis, maybe, but not chicken breast. Menus featured mackerel (not holy) served as a pâté on oatcakes; toasties, which consisted of sliced ham and black pickled something; and a sandwich called egg mayonnaise, which we'd just call egg salad. One place served pichards on toast and prawns on baked potato, but we chickened out, so to speak, and got fish 'n' chips.

They had white coffee, filtered coffee, and royal coffee, but what they didn't have was good coffee. Ick! It was a tea-drinkers paradise, but for poor Bill, my own Mr. Coffee, it was a long ten days. Every cup of java he drank was worse than the last one, and thick enough to stain his teeth black in a week. We should have brought our own Maxwell House.

And our own umbrellas. Hadn't we heard Mel Gibson say, "It's good Scottish weather—the rain is falling straight down"? Where were our heads? In the rain. It showered on our honeymoon, too, but we cuddled under one small umbrella and thought it all very romantic. Now we were cruising for a Woolworth store where we could each buy our own golf-size umbrella, an easy feat in a country where golf is so popular it's simply called, "the game."

The Long and Narrow Road

Most of our 1,350-mile adventure was spent on one-lane roads, which appeared to have been created by pouring out asphalt at the top of the hill and letting it find its own trail to the bottom. Imagine driving in the rain at twilight, with an ancient stone wall on one side, a sheer cliff leading to a loch hundreds of feet below on the other side, two nursing lambs with their mother in the middle of the road, and a car coming the other direction, driving faster than, ah, might be prudent.

The most frequently heard phrase in our car was "Waaa!" Soon, though, we got the hang of it. Turnouts along absurdly narrow roads allowed one car to pull aside while the other passed by. Very civilized, really, these lay-bys. When an oncoming car blinked its lights, it meant, "I can wait, you go first." Or as we Kentuckians translate it, "Y'all come on ahead."

The urban routes were much more dangerous. Arrows were painted on the road to show us when to merge, which was very disconcerting when we found them pointed straight at us. Traffic circles had us spinning around and going back in the direction we'd already traveled. Routes were rarely marked, with mere finger signs at intersections pointing in six different directions and written in Gaelic.

The tension was mounting when we hit Ayrshire—and missed the bus. Not missed catching it, mind you, missed *hitting* it. Broadside. To this day, we can't agree whether it was Bill's navigating or my driving that put us between a rock and a Greyhound. Here's where the diminutive size of European cars comes in handy. We squeaked through, with only the angry blast of the bus horn to haunt us. Thank you, Lord, and sorry about that woman's snapdragons.

Speaking of plant life, please note that the only heather we saw was at the gift shop, not on the Highland moors.

But we saw lots of other Scottish flora, fauna, and the like. On the far western shores of Kilchoan, we met our first midges— teensy gnatish bugs that buzz like bees and appear out of nowhere. One minute you're alone, and the next minute you have midges all over you, buzzing around your head, in your ears, up your nose. In no time your teeth look like the grillwork of a Maserati after a cross-country race.

And while there are definitely midges in Scotland, there are not monsters lurking in the lochs. We checked. Went to both of the Loch Ness tourist traps—one was the "original" museum and the other was the "official" museum—and both were pulling our wee legs. Great souvenirs, though, if you like tartan-trimmed teacups and chanters made in China.

The wild life was much more interesting at a local dining establishment (I'd say *pub* but this is a squeaky-clean book, remember), where at 9:30 one Friday night (May 25, to be exact), a local group of musicians gathered for a *ceilidh*, the Scots version of a hoedown.

They certainly gave it their all, they did. Perhaps they shouldn't have convened in a pub and sampled the wares so regularly. The small, multigenerational ensemble labored away on two accordions (which Bill says is three too many), a guitar, an electric keyboard, and a hand-drum called a *bodhran*, none of them tuned to the same pitch. We kept hoping they'd stop playing and have a good argle-bargle, since their voices were much more musical than their instruments.

The next morning we marveled at the Bay of the Pledge on Ardnamurachan (Gaelic for *gesundheit*), which is the spot where the Highlanders pledged their support to Bonnie Prince Charlie centuries ago. The sheer cliff dropped hundreds of feet to the water below, which is why we found it interesting that a sign was posted at the edge of the precipice that stated No CARS BEYOND THIS POINT.

Was this a problem in the past? we wondered. Cars plunging to certain death on the rocks below, just because they'd noticed a little rust at their temples?

Then again, while catching the ferry to the Isle of Skye, a gentleman parked his car in the queue to board the ferry and then wandered off, leaving all of us stuck behind him when the ferry arrived for loading. Apparently cars in Scotland do need their own signs to offset the neglect shown by careless owners.

Our last day in Great Britain found us rubbernecking on our way to the airport in Manchester, trying to determine why two policemen (the first bobbies we'd seen in ten days) had parked their cars nose to nose near a stone fence. Had there been an accident? Should we call the breakdown merchant? Would any panels need beating, perhaps?

Suddenly the morning mist lifted and the scene became quite clear: A cow had wandered onto the sidewalk, and the bobbies had him boxed in between two patrol cars and a stone fence.

What a fitting end to Bill and Liz's Excellent Adventure, all duly recorded in my humor journal, which, as you can see, I milked for all it was worth. Throughout those ten days in Scotland, the beautiful mountains of the Highlands and gentle hills of the Lowlands, echoed our joy-filled laughter. Even wet to the skin, we smiled like the sun.

Trust me, I've got it in writing.

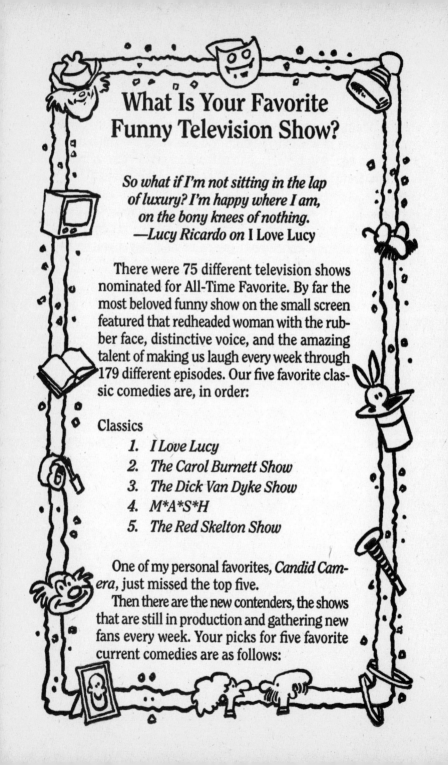

What Is Your Favorite Funny Television Show?

So what if I'm not sitting in the lap of luxury? I'm happy where I am, on the bony knees of nothing.
—Lucy Ricardo on I Love Lucy

There were 75 different television shows nominated for All-Time Favorite. By far the most beloved funny show on the small screen featured that redheaded woman with the rubber face, distinctive voice, and the amazing talent of making us laugh every week through 179 different episodes. Our five favorite classic comedies are, in order:

Classics

1. *I Love Lucy*
2. *The Carol Burnett Show*
3. *The Dick Van Dyke Show*
4. *M*A*S*H*
5. *The Red Skelton Show*

One of my personal favorites, *Candid Camera,* just missed the top five.

Then there are the new contenders, the shows that are still in production and gathering new fans every week. Your picks for five favorite current comedies are as follows:

Currents

1. *Seinfeld (Gonna miss ya!)*
2. *Home Improvement*
3. *Mad About You*
4. *3rd Rock from the Sun*
5. *Frasier*

There is no such thing as a *comedy star*. It's a contradiction in terms. A comedian has to be somebody people can relate to.

—Jerry Seinfeld

PART TWO

Seven Types of Laughter

Why do people laugh in the first place? It doesn't have to be the obvious reason—because we think something is amusing. Off the top of my head (and from the bottom of my heart), here are seven reasons why I think we laugh:

1 We're polite
2 We're clueless
3. We're nervous
4 We're relieved
5. We're frustrated
6 We're tickled (literally
7 We're amuse(

In this part of the book we will look at the different laughs that result from these situations—the polite laugh, the clueless laugh, the nervous laugh, the relieved laugh, the frustrated laugh, the tickled laugh, and the amused laugh, each with its own chapter.

Chapter 3

🐝

The Polite Laugh:
Grin and Bear It

*Politeness is one half good nature
and the other half good lying.*
—Mary Wilson Little

What's a *polite laugh*? It's the laugh we offer on cue. When it's clearly our turn, we make the appropriate noise, especially if the person trying to be funny is someone we hope to impress. No matter how faint their little quip, out comes our polite, political laugh.

Heh-heh-heh.

Our lips are curled upward, sound comes out, but nothing moves below the chin. That's the polite laugh.

It's almost always a welcome sound. The writer of Proverbs reminds us of the value of saying the right thing at the right time:

*A man has joy by the answer of his mouth,
And a word spoken in due season, how good it is!
(Proverbs 15:23)*

Indeed, a well-timed word—or a polite laugh—is a social skill worth cultivating.

For a teenage girl, the person she's giggling politely for might be a boy she's had a crush on for weeks. (Please tell me girls still have crushes, yes?) Or it could be the new Latin teacher she's buttering up so he'll score her test on a grading curve the size of Mount Vesuvius. Before the eruption.

When you hit the workaday world, polite, political laughter is the rule of the day. The CEO makes a comment with a spoonful of humor hidden among all the corporate hyperbole? *Ha-ha-ha.* It's expected. A client makes a significant contribution to your bottom line, then shares a supposedly funny story? *He-he-he.* It's necessary.

And on Sunday mornings, when the minister in the pulpit sneaks in a little smiler, we shower him with polite laughter, grateful for his efforts to bring levity along with Leviticus. *Ho-ho-ho.* It's a blessing.

The polite laugh is the sound we make when we hear an old joke and the joke teller hits the punch line. Even when we know what's coming, we hit the HA button at the appropriate moment.

Q: Why did the elephant cross the road?
A: It was the chicken's day off.

It's a timing thing, and clearly it's your turn. *Ha-ha-ha.*

Polite laughter comes in two forms: (1) A slight noise when you know something is expected of you, even if at heart you don't find the comment particularly funny, or (2) the polite grin that masks a less genteel *grrraaakkk!* that's dying to get out but which good manners won't allow.

That second kind of politically correct behavior was at work when Deanna from Kentucky went on a memorable date two decades ago.

Pasta Prima Vera Funny

Deanna's date was several years her senior, well-established in his career and much more sophisticated and dashing than her usual dates. Much to her chagrin, he suggested his favorite place for dinner—an Italian restaurant. Deanna confesses, "I don't know about other women, but I think eating spaghetti, particularly before you know someone well enough to comfortably make a mess of yourself, is a daunting task."

Daunting is an understatement. I always wear a busy print when I eat Italian cuisine, and I still end up at the dry cleaner's the next day. I don't even have to tell them where the spot is. Bill says food falls at right angles when I'm wearing a dry-clean-only outfit. And Italian food is the worst culprit of all.

Deanna was dressed to the nines. Actually, to the seventies— a navy three-piece suit and a satin, pale-baby-blue blouse with a long flowing tie that knotted at the neck and hung the length of her torso.

Yes, we remember those.

"Throughout the meal I was most prim and proper, carefully twirling my spaghetti on the spoon, taking ridiculously small bites, and delicately touching the corners of my lips with my napkin while attempting to sneak swabs at the rest of my mouth.

"My date sat across from me at this elegant restaurant and grinned for no reason whatsoever. I decided he must have fallen for me hard. Just as I finished my meal, I reached into my lap to get the napkin I'd used to wipe my mouth and discovered— horrors!—that the cloth napkin had gotten under my pale-blue satin tie and that I had used my tie as a napkin! It was covered with bright red lipstick and pasta sauce. No wonder he was grinning."

Ah, but politely so.

Awkward situations like this often produce polite laughter, since it's slightly more acceptable than sobbing hysterically, screaming in terror, or running in the opposite direction. What poses as polite laughter may simply be a cover-up for the full-tilt explosion we're holding back until a more appropriate moment.

Dog Bites Man in the Funny Bone

Sharon from Ohio had a surprise for her veterinarian. Sharon's beloved dog had been very ill, and the family made numerous trips and calls to the vet before having to end the dog's suffering. Sharon's first child was due about a month later, which helped to ease the pain of losing their dog and gave them something thrilling to look forward to.

The evening of their blessed event finally arrived. As her husband got things ready for the hospital, Sharon excitedly called the doctor's office. A very poised answering-service attendant answered the phone. When Sharon proudly announced that her water had broken and that she would need to meet the doctor at the hospital, the woman politely replied, "Honey, unless you're having a litter, I'm afraid Dr. Smith can't help you. You've called your veterinarian."

Bobbie, our South Australian contributor who has a son with autism, offered another example of polite laughter. Along with her son's particular disability goes a very loud voice with no volume control. He was nearly six feet tall when she took him on his favorite holiday treat to buy ice cream.

As Bobbie tells it, "We joined a large crowd of mothers, aunties, grandmothers, and small children, all there for the same reason. While we were waiting, a pregnant woman passed by us, which brought to my son's mind a book he had thoroughly read and committed to memory, *How Babies Are Made*."

It seems he could recite it word for word.

"His loud voice boomed over the assembled gathering. 'We don't know what it's going to be, Mum. It all depends on what's between its legs. If it's like mine it's a boy, if it's like yours it's a girl.'

"Slowly, quietly, the stunned crowd melted away and we were left to confront the two young assistants who appeared to be in dire straits. We got our ice cream quickly, then made our way down a side alley to the car while my son continued with the rest of the narrative from his book." In polite but full voice, of course. The polite thing to do in this scenario is swallow one's laugh—hook, line, and sinker—right along with the ice cream.

Know When to Fold 'Em

Recently I got myself in a pickle, and I watched Bill try very hard not to be impolite and laugh out loud. We were on a long trip, and I'd brought my laptop computer with me to get some writing done.

Understand, when it comes to bodies, I've been, uh, abundantly blessed. But laptop manufacturers must have a one-size-fits-all lap in mind because this thing does not stay on my lap—it slides off the end of my knees. That's not a problem at home or in hotels where it sits on a desk. In the van, however, I have to prop my long legs up on our elongated dashboard to make a desktop. It isn't very graceful looking, but it works like a charm at night when no one can see inside the van.

The kids were fast asleep, a CD of soft Celtic music was playing, and I was tapping away at my keyboard when I suddenly decided to recline my seat ever so slightly so I could have even more lap room. The seat snapped back faster and farther than I expected, which sent me scooting forward, dangerously close to the edge of the seat.

Gravity now began taking its toll on my carefully positioned "desk." My legs began pointing due north. The computer slipped onto my tummy, making it difficult to move without the risk of my expensive equipment tumbling onto the car floor. Sitting up was out of the question, as I had no leverage by this point.

My round bottom was responding to the inevitable and heading toward the floor. Imagine a fan, half open, slowly but surely being squeezed closed. Nose to knees, I started folding up while Bill, driving along a dark highway at sixty miles per hour, was unable to help me.

Not that he could've anyway, the rat. I could tell by his breathing that he was stifling a laugh that threatened to fill the car. I did the polite thing and laughed first.

Haawww!

Set free from his inhibitions by my own explosion, Bill did his best to keep breathing and driving, while I just tried to keep breathing with a laptop pinned to my diaphragm and no relief in sight. Finally we pulled into a gas station. There was nothing to do but have Bill open the door on my side, rescue the laptop, yank me out of the bottom of the car, and unfold me onto the pavement.

The people milling around the gas pumps were very polite. They didn't start laughing until we pulled back onto the highway. We could see them in the rearview mirror—bent over, throwing their hands in the air, shrieking.

Let's face it, it's hard to use a laptop computer when you don't have a lap!

Who Do You Think You're Talking To?

One final story about a daughter who didn't mean to sound cruel. Honest.

Jeanne's daughter moved to a small town that didn't have a recycling program. She'd been used to saving her recyclables, so she continued to do so and asked her mother to take them along home with her whenever she visited.

One day when Jeanne visited, they loaded a huge sackful in her trunk just before she left. When Jeanne headed down the street, her daughter waved good-bye and turned to her husband, who'd just strolled out of the house.

"Boy," she sighed in relief. "Am I glad to get rid of that old bag!"

He looked at his wife in shock. How could she speak about her mother like that?! It took some time to sort it all out, and the family still laughs about Jeanne, the Old Bag, and her daughter who had no intention of being impolite.

Chapter 4

The Clueless Laugh: Never Fight a Battle of Wits with an Unarmed Man

It takes a lot of things to prove you are smart, but only one thing to prove you are ignorant.
—Don Herold

We not only laugh to be polite. We also laugh because we haven't the faintest idea what's going on. I call it the *clueless laugh*. It's how we respond when we're confused, don't have all the facts, or want people to think we're "in the loop" when in truth we haven't even seen the loop since 1983.

Laurie from North Carolina watched a homeless Siamese cat in her backyard for a few weeks. She began to feed it, hoping to catch the cat and find its owner. "I saw it crawl into a pile of wood and went outside with a bowl of food to try to coax it to come to me. I stood for several minutes with the bowl in my hand calling, 'Here kitty, here kitty,' not realizing that I was being observed by a man next door digging a new gas line."

He couldn't stand it any longer, turned off the backhoe, and walked over to her. "Lady," he explained, "you don't have to coax that woodpile to eat—it's dead already!"

I'm not sure if he thought she was crazy or if she decided he was a little off. Forrest Gump would say, "Stupid is as stupid does," but then again, what does that mean, anyway?!

Time for the clueless laugh.

Illogical but Lovable

Gracie Allen was a master at the non sequitur (Latin for "it does not follow"). She may have appeared clueless, but don't you believe it. She was a woman with a steel-trap mind, brilliantly disguised as a beautiful airhead.

Gracie would have been proud of this unintentional non sequitur from pregnant Pam:

Shari from Nevada loves celebrating her birthday on June 21, officially the longest day of the year. When her friend, Pam, was expecting a baby around that time, Shari tried to convince Pam that the twenty-first would be the perfect day to deliver.

Pam looked her square in the eye and said, "Why would I want to be in labor on the longest day of the year?"

Duh.

And Duh One, and Duh Two

The fifth-grade class at my son Matthew's school has a perfect method for handling all those ignorant moments in our lives: Each student is permitted one *duh* per day.

I'm not sure one duh would hold me, but I suppose I could stockpile them on good days, in case I ever needed five in a row.

Like the song says, "Here are a few of my favorite duhs . . ." It's only fair that I share one of my own duh moments first.

Duh #1: One of my dear friends in speaking, Sue Thomas, is a consummate pro on the platform—and is also profoundly deaf. While visiting in Louisville, she spoke at my children's school for their chapel service. I'd spoken there myself, and I knew how hard it was to keep the attention of several hundred kids, kindergarten through fifth grade, as they wiggled all over the gym.

"Were they quiet for you?" I asked Sue, careful to look in her direction so she could read my lips.

With a perfectly straight face and a twinkle in her eye, she said, "Oh, yes. They were very quiet."

Duhhh, Liz!

Duh #2: Jennifer from California was busy at work coming up with a new letterhead style for her company. Her head was filled with design ideas, which is why when the phone rang, she answered it, "Pleasant Valley Hospital, this is letterhead."

Duh #3: Albert from Kentucky had just started his new job as an assistant county farm agent. They had a training session for all the 4-H club officers in the county, including a practice meeting to learn parliamentary procedures.

The president said, "We will now have the reading of the minutes."

The secretary looked puzzled at first, then checked his watch and announced, "Looks like about twenty after."

(Albert confesses the real duh is on him, since he was the one who trained the secretaries.)

Duh #4: After a long day at work, Ginny came home for a late dinner, turned on the television, and was cleaning up the kitchen when the phone rang.

"I've been wondering where you and Rick were," laughed her good friend on the other end of the line.

Thinking she was being funny, Ginny bantered back and forth with her until her friend finally said, "No, I mean it, where are you?"

"In the kitchen," Ginny answered, confused. "Where are *you*?"

"I'm on my cell phone on your back porch. I've been pounding the door and ringing the bell for five minutes!"

Duh #5: Modern communication technology doesn't guarantee that the message gets through. Even years after Beverly's mother passed away, the family still received a piece of mail addressed to her. Her sister wrote DECEASED across the envelope and returned it to the sender.

A new letter was promptly sent, addressed to Lois E. Deceased.

Foreign Matters

Melissa moved north from Wilmington, North Carolina, to Raleigh, where the weather is decidedly colder. Her parents, Becky and Fred, visited her there and noticed in the parking lot of her apartment complex a sign that featured a picture of a faucet dripping and the words FREEZE WARNING. LEAVE WATER DRIPPING.

Fred, being the dutiful father, asked, "Melissa, did you leave your water dripping in the apartment?"

A look of total confusion crossed Melissa's face. "What does the water in my apartment have to do with the water in the parking lot?"

"Honey, what do you think that sign means?"

"The water dripping from the leaves causes the parking lot to freeze, so you need to be careful driving. Right?"

Far be it from me to throw the first stone. I'm the woman who just got back from Germany, including repeated trips up and down the autobahn near Frankfurt. Signs pointing to many familiar cities kept popping up along the busy, high-speed highway—Heidelberg, Koln, Munich—but I was amazed how many times we turned off a road with a sign pointing to Ausfahrt.

I finally got the nerve to ask my bilingual driver, "This Ausfahrt must be a very big place."

She grinned from ear to ear. "Oh, all roads lead to ausfahrt."

"But, I've never even heard of that city!" I protested.

"Oh, you have *ausfahrt* in the states too," she insisted. "It means 'exit.'"

There went my duh for September 10.

Ann from Vermont visited Germany by mail, since her in-laws lived there. As a new bride, she wanted to write them and describe all their wedding gifts. Dictionary in hand, Ann started to list their wedding presents—casserole dishes, a hamper, blankets, cooking utensils, all easily found in her English/German dictionary.

Then she came to toaster. Hmm. No word for *toaster*.

She found German words for *electric, toast,* and *maker,* which came out *electrisch trinkspoof fabricans.* When her new husband came home, she proudly showed him her list. He laughed until tears ran down his face. Finally, he explained that their toaster was now "an electric man at a wedding making a toast to the bride and groom."

Caution! Unplug toaster before giving electric man a drink.

The language barrier works both ways, of course. Sally in Ramstein was amused by the German businessman who had cards printed in English for his American customers: AFTER YOU BUY NINE CAR WASHES, YOU BECOME ONE FREE.

English Bloopers

Even when we stick with English, we can say one thing and mean another. Deanna from Indiana described the breakfast scene at her house one morning. Her father was trying to discuss something with her mother who was mumbling to herself while adjusting the toaster button and not listening to him at all.

Finally he said in disgust, "Where is your mind?"

Still turning the light-dark button, her mother responded, "I think it's on medium."

My friend Sue is a missionary in France, where many things are outrageously expensive—a gallon of gas costs about four dollars. She admits, "Now that I've lived out of the country for thirteen years, I've almost completely lost touch with what things cost in the U.S. and tend to think that American expenses are so low."

When Sue and her family were home on furlough, a family member took them all shopping at her expense. Sue's husband absolutely insisted that they pay for lunch at McDonald's, knowing he had twenty U.S. dollars in his wallet. Surely that would be enough to cover lunch for six at a hamburger joint, right?

You know the rest of this story. He had to borrow another ten dollars from their generous family member or consider becoming a kitchen missionary at Mickey D's.

Leigh Ann remembers well the day her parents bought their first dishwasher. Her father liked to inspect every new thing that came into their house, so he stayed in the kitchen and watched the display count down all forty-four minutes of the dishwashing cycle.

As Leigh Ann tells it, "I was upstairs with my mother and older sister when my dad came running up the stairs shouting, 'The dishwasher is useless; it's useless!'

"The three of us looked at one another, amazed that our newest appliance would be broken after only one use, but he insisted that because we had a water softener, the dishwasher was useless."

She decided to look for herself, and there it was, on the inside door, next to the detergent dispenser: USE LESS WITH SOFT WATER.

Mechanically Challenged

Vicki from North Carolina was washing cars, not dishes—
or at least she was trying to. She couldn't get her car on the
tracks that would pull her car into the wash bay. "I missed the
tracks and my car was poking way up in the air, so high I
couldn't even get out of the car. I kept blowing the horn until
the manager came out."

He took one look at her car, pointed skyward, and said, "How
on earth did you do this?" After helping her step down out of
the car, the frustrated man told her, "Just stay out of the way."

"Did I hurt my car?"

"No!" He got the car down on the tracks and washed it himself, much to her chagrin.

The next time Vicki visited a car wash—a different one—
she was driving back and forth, back and forth, trying to hit
the track, when a nice man waiting behind her, dressed in his
Sunday suit, got out of his car and stepped in front of hers to
direct her. Seconds later, the wash cycle started and water came
pouring down on the nice man in his nice suit.

How about we chip in and buy Vicki a bucket?

Splish Splash

Even trying to get myself clean proves to be a humbling experience. I was staying at a snazzy older hotel in Illinois. The gray, chilly weather outside was quickly forgotten when I saw the cozy fireplace in my room, the tall poster bed draped in a thick, downy comforter, and the luxurious terry-cloth robe hanging in the closet.

But the real surprise was the Jacuzzi in the exquisitely appointed bathroom. Amid mirrored walls and marble floors rose an oversize beauty of a tub, jets at the ready. A whole basket of fancy bath products sat perched on the edge, inviting me to indulge in an afternoon bubble bath.

I didn't have a presentation until much later that day. So, why not?

I followed the directions to the letter, pushing the silver button to start the jets at the appropriate time and giggling to myself at the last instruction on the posted sign: IF PREGNANT, SEE YOUR DOCTOR FIRST. Hmm. Wouldn't your husband be the more likely suspect? *Tee-hee.*

I eased down into the steaming water, feeling the cares of the world slide off my shoulders. This is it; we're buying one of these. Tomorrow.

Using the loofah the hotel generously provided, I lathered it up with a big dollop of almond-and-aloe foaming gel and scrubbed it into my skin. If you've grown an aloe plant, you know this is pretty slimy stuff, like okra, or worse. Soon I was one slick chick, sliding around the tub feeling wonderfully relaxed and silky smooth, ready to dry off and get dressed for my program.

I scooted m feet under me and tried to grab the edges of the bathtub   faint sense of foreboding crawled up my spine. The tub was surrounded with a foot-wide flat edge of marble, and there were glass walls on three sides. In other words, nothing to hang on to. My feet shot back out from under me—kersplash!—and I displaced a few gallons of sudsy water, sending them spilling over onto the marble floor.

Maybe a tiny woman could have slithered her way out of this dilemma without incident, but this woman of substance was in trouble.

I tried pulling myself over the edge, seal-like, but feared creating a tidal wave that would engulf my dry clothes draped mere feet away. I considered draining the tub, but then worried about slipping and cracking my cranium wide open, thereby missing my evening program, my family, and the rest of my life. I toyed with filling the tub to the tippy-top, then spilling over the edge with the first few bubbles. I would drown in the process, of course, but at least I'd be out of the tub.

Looking around desperately, panic tightening my throat, I spied a possible solution across the room—a telephone, the latest accessory for swanky bathrooms. Hmm. Whom would I call? "Hello, Front Desk? Could you send a weight lifter to Room 207? That's right. Oh, and blindfold him first, okay?"

The water was getting chilly, and time was quickly ticking by. Slippery or not, I had to get out of that tub. I slithered one leg over the edge and started pushing against the opposite side of the tub. Like a submarine surfacing on the sea at a 45-degree angle, I aimed my leg northeast and shoved my arms southwest and prayed the maid wouldn't pick that exact moment to appear for turndown service.

Before I was fully seated on the marble edge, there was one precarious moment when I could have gone either way—falling back to certain disaster or splashing out with the tsunami— but the Lord smiled on my sorry state and guided me safely, if not gracefully, to the fuzzy rug below.

A sudden knock at the door had me scrambling for the hotel's terry-cloth robe. "Who is it?"

A muffled voice responded, "We've had a report of water dripping in Room 107 below yours. Is there a problem with the Jacuzzi?"

I buried my face in a towel to stifle a loud guffaw. "Gee, a problem?" I sang out. "I haven't got a clue."

Chapter 5

The Nervous Laugh: It's Hard to Laugh Up Your Sleeve When You're Wearing Your Birthday Suit

I could see that, if not actually disgruntled,
he was far from being gruntled.
—P. G. Wodehouse

We laugh to be polite, we laugh because we're clueless, and we laugh because we're nervous and hope to shake off our anxiety with a high-pitched, uncontrollable giggle I call the *nervous laugh*.

See the bride at the altar with her veil bobbing up and down? She could be crying, but it's more likely that she's gotten a case of the giggles, brought on by sheer terror. Nothing genuinely funny may be happening, but when you're strung tighter than a violin string, it doesn't take much to make you vibrate with laughter.

The minister stumbles over a word? *Tee-hee-hee.*

Your groom has his cuff links on backwards? *Tee-hee-hee.*

The flame on your unity candle just snuffed itself out? *Tee-hee-hee.*

The more fear involved in a situation, the more our mind and body demand some form of release from the tension. We might shiver with fright (like heroines always do in mystery novels), or we might quiver with unexpected—even inappropriate—laughter as we try to cope with some anxiety-producing circumstance.

Years ago, I came across a list of the top ten things people fear most:

1. Speaking to a group
2. Heights
3. Insects
4. Money problems
5. Deep water
6. Sickness
7. Death
8. Flying
9. Loneliness
10. Dogs

As a professional speaker, I believe it's possible to experience all ten of these fears simultaneously.

Suppose that **speaking to groups** is part of your job description and that those who are **higher up** have been **bugging** you to do more speaking. Since you don't want to **lose your income** and therefore get into **deep water** at home, you step up to the platform, feeling **ill** and **scared to death**, especially when your notes go **flying** off the lectern. You realize you've never felt so **alone** and forlorn because you know this speech you're about to present is a real **dog**.

See? And you thought you had a few fears to deal with.

The Bible says, "Perfect love casts out fear."

So true. And I might add, a perfect *laugh* casts out fear too. Our contributors had a plethora of phobias to conquer with humor, including a fear of flies, snakes, and guns, or a fear of some awful thing happening to them, like fainting in public or being robbed.

When Cathy was four years old, she was scared silly of flies. A common little housefly was more terrifying to her than the nastiest beast or the darkest night on earth. One day while she was riding her tricycle, a fly landed next to her and she started wailing.

Cathy's mother decided she'd had enough. She sat at the picnic table with Cathy and convinced her to wait for a fly to land. When a fly dutifully showed up, Cathy's mother told her to take a good close look and encouraged her that nothing bad would happen if she did.

Cathy got as close as she could to the horrible creature, then raised her head to joyfully announce, "That fly has little pink pedal pushers on!" She was never afraid of flies again.

It's not clear what kind of drug Cathy's mother slipped into her child's lemonade to make her see pink pedal pushers on the fly, but the key is, humor helped Cathy laugh away her fears.

When Eve Met the Snake, She Wasn't Dressed Either

It was a hot, dry summer on Betty and Lloyd's Kansas farm, so hot that everyone was looking for a cool, shady place to camp out, including the snakes. Betty lived in an old rock house, and they were in the process of adding a bathroom. One evening as she was toweling off after a refreshing bath in the unfinished bathroom, Betty heard something scritch, scritching across the bathroom floor.

Glancing in the direction of the noise, she spotted a spine-tingling, fear-inducing sight: A snake was headed right for her! With a leap and a bound that would put Superman to shame, she raced through the bedroom, dining room, and kitchen and was out the door, across the porch, and to the end of the walk, where her husband intercepted her mad dash.

Betty admits, "Coming to my senses, I realized I did not have on a stitch of clothing. Modesty overcoming fear, I sheepishly and cautiously went back in the house, covered myself with a tea towel, and perched on the kitchen table until Lloyd disposed of the harmless garden snake."

Were her troubles over? Of course not. She began fretting about their neighbors, John and Mattie, who lived across the road. Had they been sitting on their screened-in porch? Betty's exit had been fast but far from quiet. Had she attracted their attention?

She would soon find out, since she worked with Mattie. She avoided her at work the next day, and instead described her great snake adventure to her best friend, Wilma, including her fear that she might have provided a free "peep" show for her neighbors.

Betty explains, "Wilma soothed me as a good friend would and assured me she would discreetly find out if Mattie was aware of any goings-on at our house. Lunchtime came, and Wilma gave me the bad news. Mattie and John had been sitting on the porch. They heard the shrieks and saw the whole thing."

Betty avoided her neighbors for the next few weeks until one day Wilma finally confessed the truth: Mattie knew nothing, heard nothing, and saw nothing!

I think I'd be more afraid of Wilma than a garden snake.

Hired Gun

Linda from Colorado laughs every time she sees their custom-made gun cabinet, remembering how it ended up in their house. Her father-in-law, a member of the Texas Cattleman's Association, had purchased a beautiful commemorative rifle that was engraved with his ranch's brand as well as other historic Texas brands. Hubby Paul had often admired the rifle, and when his dad offered it to him, Paul was beside himself with joy.

The first thing Paul did was call a local cabinetmaker and ask him if could design a special display case for it. The cabinetmaker agreed but forgot about the conversation. A few weeks later, Paul called the cabinetmaker back, rifle in hand, and blurted out, "Hi, this is Paul—"

The cabinetmaker missed the introduction and only heard an excited stranger say, "—I've got a gun and I'm coming over." Terrified, the cabinetmaker anxiously awaited the unknown gunman's arrival, mentally reviewing his list of clients, trying to decide if any of them felt disgruntled about their new cabinets.

When teddy-bearlike Paul showed up with the commemorative rifle, you can bet the cabinetmaker breathed a laugh of relief.

"Stop, Thief"

He wasn't the Jason of *Friday the 13th* fame, but for Ann from Texas this Jason was just as ominous. Ann's husband advertised two big-ticket items in their local newspaper. Ann told him she wanted no part selling these items because (1) she'd heard horror stories of strangers calling and coming to your home, and (2) the items were stereo speakers and a workout gym that she knew virtually nothing about. He assured her he'd handle it all.

The phone immediately started ringing. An extremely polite young man named Jason showed up on their doorstep to look at the speakers. The two men agreed on $450 for the speakers, but Jason would not have the full amount till payday on Friday. He left a twenty-dollar deposit, and they arranged a pickup time.

On Wednesday, Jason called while her husband was at work and explained he'd gotten the money early and wanted to pick up the speakers that evening. Ann's mind raced. "I did not want to do this, and knowing he would arrive shortly after dark made me more leery. I thought about alerting our neighborhood twenty-four-hour police patrol that I was having this stranger come over, but I decided I was just being paranoid."

At 8:30, Jason appeared and handed her a wad of money folded in half. "I'm two dollars short. Can I give it to you in quarters?"

She held out her hand, not counting the wad in her other hand, but sliding the corners enough to see that it looked like four hundred dollar bills, two tens, a five, and some ones. Within minutes the speakers were loaded in his Jeep and Jason was out their driveway and gone.

Ann counted the money more carefully and discovered to her horror that while a normal-looking Ben Franklin bill was folded in half on the outside of the wad, inside the other three hundreds were odd. The face of old Ben was huge, not centered on the bill. *It is counterfeit money!* she realized. *It isn't even a good forgery job; it is blatantly fake.*

"It was Monopoly money and I'd fallen for it," Ann moaned to herself. "I was diverted by the old count-the-quarter scam." She grabbed the phone and called their neighborhood security, frantically describing the vehicle and the criminal who'd just left her house. They told her to call 911 and alert the city police, which soon had officers searching the main roads leading out of their subdivision and the closest pawn-shop locations.

Ann's head was spinning, thinking about the criminal who would undoubtedly return to rob them any minute. She paged her husband repeatedly. No reply. Twenty minutes later an officer arrived at her door. Still shaken, she explained the whole story.

"This is a terrible print job," she declared. "See for yourself."

The officer looked it over, and in a very serious voice said, "Ma'am, did you know they changed the hundred-dollar bill?"

Her jaw dropped. "What?"

"About two years ago, the government changed the hundred-dollar bill."

Her face got hot and turned various shades of red. The change in currency must have occurred while they were living overseas. "Look," she stammered, "I'm a stay-at-home mom. When would I ever have my hands on a hundred-dollar bill?"

They immediately called off the manhunt for Jason, and Ann didn't bother to page her husband again. Meanwhile, fake-Ben sightings have been reported over many parts of the U.S.

Finally, Judy from Kentucky wasn't nervous or laughing, she just needed to sit down. Pregnant at the time, she was standing in line at a shopping-mall food court when she began to feel dizzy and light-headed. She walked a few steps but suddenly got tunnel vision. She knew she was going to faint.

She grabbed the first handy chair, sat down, and put her head between her legs for several minutes. When she sat up, she realized that she'd joined an elderly couple at their lunch table. She apologized and tried to stand up, but felt dizzy again. Not wanting to stay at their table all day, she dragged a chair across the mall and *sat* in line until her food was ready. Someone called security. "Either to make sure I was okay or because they thought I was a nut."

No way, not unless she tried to pay for her lunch with a hundred dollar bill featuring Big Ben's off-center face.

When fear and apprehension strike, your funny bone is your most powerful weapon.

Chapter 6

The Relieved
Laugh:
By Jovial!

A good time to laugh is anytime you can.
—*Linda Ellerbee*

Okay, so you're not polite, clueless, or nervous. Then why are you laughing? Ohh, I get it. Whew!

You're relieved.

The *relieved laugh* comes out in a breathy *woosh*. You probably weren't even aware you were under that much tension when suddenly out of nowhere the situation resolves itself and—*Ha!*—you feel decidedly better.

Eilene from Maine longed for a little relief from the embarrassment she felt while visiting a school and orphanage in Kenya. Dozens of children who spoke only Swahili pressed around her, trying to see if the white of her skin would rub off. They were all yelling "Jumbo!" and "Super!"

Eilene grumbled to her interpreter, "I know I need to lose weight, but I didn't think I was that fat and large."

He burst out laughing, then explained, "In Swahili, *jumbo* means 'hello' and *super* means 'hello very much.'"

What a relief. I thought Jumbo was an elephant.

The Key to the Crime

Whenever I misplace something, I find I always laugh when I find it (unless looking for it makes me late, in which case the sounds I make are nothing at all like laughter).

Pat shared the time a coworker was carrying a single, loose, office key in her dress pocket, then later in the day realized it was missing. They tried retracing her steps for almost an hour and were about to give up when the woman turned and walked away—and revealed the missing key, safely trapped inside her pantyhose, plastered against her left calf.

Pat says, "Now whenever anything is missing at work, we do a pantyhose check."

What if the missing item is a filing cabinet?

Shop 'Til You . . .

Jan from Nevada can laugh with relief now, but I'd love to have seen the look on her face when it happened. She and her hubby-to-be were on a skiing jaunt together and stopped at a minimarket on the way for snacks.

Her man was standing in front of her in line when she saw some goodies that she wanted and stepped away to gather them from the shelves, not knowing her honey had gone off to do the same thing.

Like any dating couple, they were affectionate in public, so when she turned back in line, she put her hand on his bottom and gave it an affectionate caress. As Pat tells it, "I was shocked when this strange man turned around and looked at me." Meanwhile, the man destined to become her husband saw the whole thing, along with half the customers, who were all laughing.

The man she mistook for her boyfriend said to her, "Wow, lady. At first I thought you were trying to steal my wallet, but the truth is, you made my day."

Jan says her husband now calls those little markets *Grab and Go*.

It's Snowing Up North

Look, these things happen. Life's most embarrassing moments and all that. Laughing about them not only relieves your own tension, but gives everyone around you permission to giggle too. Good thing, or otherwise they might have to excuse themselves and go explode with laughter on the front porch.

Which is precisely what three Navy sailors must have desperately wanted to do when Karen served them spaghetti dinner. Karen's hubby was a Navy officer who invited three single sailors over for dinner when Karen's first child was just two months old. The house looked great, Karen served a lovely meal by candlelight, and everything was fine until she returned to the table after nursing little Ashley.

Within minutes, hubby was making frantic motions, trying to get her attention. Karen was busy serving the food and asking who wanted bread. Finally she realized that all four men were blushing and staring pointedly at her scoop-necked dress.

No wonder.

One of her nursing pads had walked its way up and out of her neckline, and was waving to everyone in sight. Karen, ever the quick thinker, swiftly pulled it out and said, "Anyone need a coaster?"

Sandy was in the midst of serving dinner when things got interesting at her house. Hamburgers were on the menu, and Sandy decided to shake the ketchup bottle. She was halfway across the kitchen, flipping her wrist side-to-side "like a baton twirler on speed," when the top flew off.

Do I need to describe this for you? A big glob of ketchup on her head, more dripping off her eyebrows and nose, ketchup on the table, the walls, the ceiling, the carpet, even on two newly upholstered yellow brocade dining-room chairs, ketchup clear into the corner of the living room and up the side of the yellow-flowered Queen Anne wing chair, and in the stereo headphones that just happened to be in the wing chair at the time.

"There was ketchup everywhere—except in the ketchup bottle." Sand confesses, "With my weirdly warped sense of humor, I promptly burst into fits of hysterical laughter, which brought the whole gang running from the living room. After they had determined that I was not mortally wounded—if I'm laughing, how serious can the injuries be?—they joined in the hilarity of the moment."

Yes, the hamburgers got cold and the chairs may never be quite so pristine a yellow again, but it makes quite a story. If everything went exactly according to plan, life would be a dull, humorless disaster.

Now it's my turn to tell a true tale of an embarrassing moment.

The Bombing of Newport Beach

February 1993. Newport Beach, California. The National Speakers Association, my peer group, was gathered for their winter educational workshop, and I was invited to be their Saturday evening speaker.

Big honor. Big blessing. Big ego alert.

Several details contributed to the outcome of this particular evening. For starters, I spoke in Columbus, Ohio, that same morning, and so had to fly out at 1:00 P.M. for the West Coast, hoping and praying my flight would land on time. I arrived at 5:00 with the main event just two hours away and my nerves stretched to the limit. Toss in a three-hour time change and a little jet lag for good measure, and you get some sense of my level of energy at this point. But it gets worse.

The huge meal (for some, with wine) took a l-o-n-g time to serve. Beef—heavy, sleep-inducing beef—was on the menu. And baked potatoes. And cheesecake. *Zzzzzzz*.

A thirty-minute slide presentation of fine art preceded my program. Oh, that perked people right up.

It was late—well after 9:00—when I stepped on the stage. By my body clock, it was midnight, as it was for many attendees.

The room was too dark, with large mirrored posts blocking both my view and theirs. Everywhere I looked, I saw Liz, and Liz looked nervous.

The five hundred attendees were, for the most part, speakers, fully capable of doing what I was about to do, and anxious to see why I was invited to do so instead of them.

If you are, say, a salesperson, this would be like having five hundred other reps standing around watching you make a sales pitch while talking among themselves—"I wouldn't do it that way, would you? Gee, I'd never have said that."

You get the idea. Pressure City.

If it sounds like I'm making excuses, you're absolutely right. Even though I'd prayed, prepared, and practiced, I laid an egg in Newport Beach. It was the longest hour I've ever spent on the platform. The few times folks did laugh, it had a strained, let's-help-her-out quality.

Groan.

One of the veterans of our association was sitting right in front of me, fast asleep, snoring away. (If I'd had a pocketful of mini-marshmallows, I'd have tossed them at his teeth like bean-bags at a clown face.)

There is no death like dying on the platform. I could feel my hair turning gray as I spoke. Everywhere I looked, I saw mirrored images of myself. Bombing.

When, blessedly, I finished the last word, the audience leaped to their feet—and ran out the door. I'd hoped for a standing ovation; this was more like a running ovation. I made a bee-line for my room, where I collapsed on the bed, crying like a baby.

It was 2:00 A.M. in Louisville, so I couldn't even call Bill for moral support.

Can you feel my pain?

I'd wanted to give them a performance they would never forget. Sure enough, I had.

Monday morning back in Kentucky, the phone in my office started ringing with words of encouragement from my peers.

"Liz, it wasn't that bad."

"I think people were just tired."

"I'd give you a 12, but the audience was a 4."

Nice try, but I knew the truth: On a scale of 1 to 10, I was the one who deserved the 4. Comedian David Brenner says when you do humor, you can't get good without bombing. But, David, did it have to be that night?!

I was licking my wounds in Louisville, certain that I'd never show my face at another Association gathering again, when the unthinkable happened. The program chair for the big National Convention in Washington, D.C., called and asked me to do a program to kick off the whole event.

I was stunned to silence. The committee members must not have been in Newport Beach.

The obvious solution was to say no thanks, but it's such an honor to be asked that speakers almost never refuse.

My heart was in my throat (or was it my shoes?). I needed help and fast, so I faxed a dear friend of mine, Rosita Perez, a consummate pro in the speaking business and the one who'd introduced me that fateful night.

"Rosita," I wrote, "how am I going to get back up on the platform? You were in Newport Beach, you saw me bomb, what am I going to do?"

She faxed me back. "Liz, you did not bomb, it just wasn't magic." (Rosita is a motivational speaker. They say things like that.) Her fax went on, "Let me ask you something: Do you like Dustin Hoffman?"

I'm thinking, *Dustin Hoffman?! Was he in Newport Beach?*

Her fax continued. "He's a brilliant actor, yes? Award-winning, an incredible talent, a Hollywood legend, yes?"

Yes, yes.

"Did you see him in *Ishtar*?"

Oh, yes, I'd seen *Ishtar*, back when I reviewed movies for a local radio station. I declared it the single worst movie I'd ever paid money to see. That distinction still stands. Forty million dollars, Warren Beatty, Dustin Hoffman—a bomb.

A big bomb.

In fact, one of my favorite cartoons from *The Far Side* showed a video store in Hades, with nothing on the shelves but *Ishtar, Ishtar, Ishtar* . . .

"So, Liz," her fax concluded, "if Dustin Hoffman can survive an *Ishtar* in his career and come back and win an Oscar for Best Actor in *Rain Man*, can't you get back up on that platform?"

The woman had me there. The more I thought about it, the more excited I got. Yes, I would get back up on that horse, and if I fell off again, at least I knew I could survive.

Inspired by her words, I sat down at my computer and created a graphic reminder of my meaningful discovery:

ISHTAR HAPPENS.

It happened to Dustin, it happened to me in Newport Beach, and when/if it happens to you, now you'll be ready. There's a Japanese proverb that says, "When you stumble, don't get up empty-handed." Indeed, if you stand up with your head full of wisdom, your heart full of laughter, and your arms full of encouraging words like Rosita's, who knows what might happen.

Are you wondering what happened in Washington, D.C.? I marched into that meeting room full of my peers, with my ISHTAR HAPPENS sign safely tucked in the back of my notebook to remind me that failing beats not trying, every time. And on a scale of 1 to 10, it was . . . well, I'll sound like I'm bragging if I say a 15, so I'll simply tell you what a delight it was to call Bill and say, "Ta-da!"

What a relief.

God doesn't have Ishtar days, but he understands them only too well. That's why he gave us laughter, so we can survive them with our sense of humor and confidence intact.

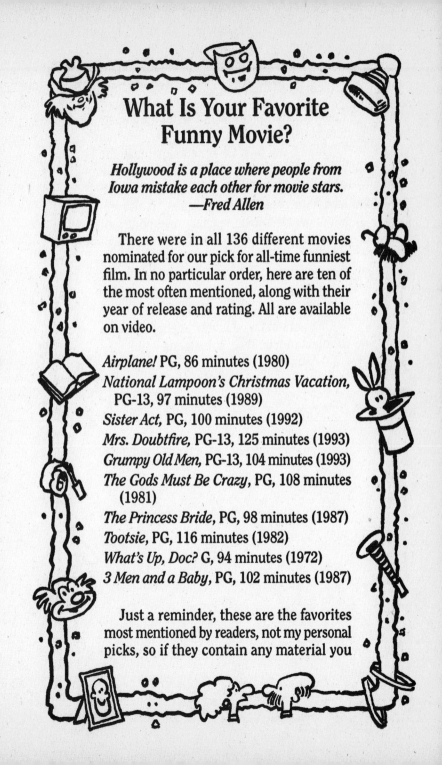

What Is Your Favorite Funny Movie?

*Hollywood is a place where people from
Iowa mistake each other for movie stars.*
—*Fred Allen*

There were in all 136 different movies
nominated for our pick for all-time funniest
film. In no particular order, here are ten of
the most often mentioned, along with their
year of release and rating. All are available
on video.

Airplane! PG, 86 minutes (1980)

National Lampoon's Christmas Vacation,
 PG-13, 97 minutes (1989)

Sister Act, PG, 100 minutes (1992)

Mrs. Doubtfire, PG-13, 125 minutes (1993)

Grumpy Old Men, PG-13, 104 minutes (1993)

The Gods Must Be Crazy, PG, 108 minutes
 (1981)

The Princess Bride, PG, 98 minutes (1987)

Tootsie, PG, 116 minutes (1982)

What's Up, Doc? G, 94 minutes (1972)

3 Men and a Baby, PG, 102 minutes (1987)

Just a reminder, these are the favorites
most mentioned by readers, not my personal
picks, so if they contain any material you

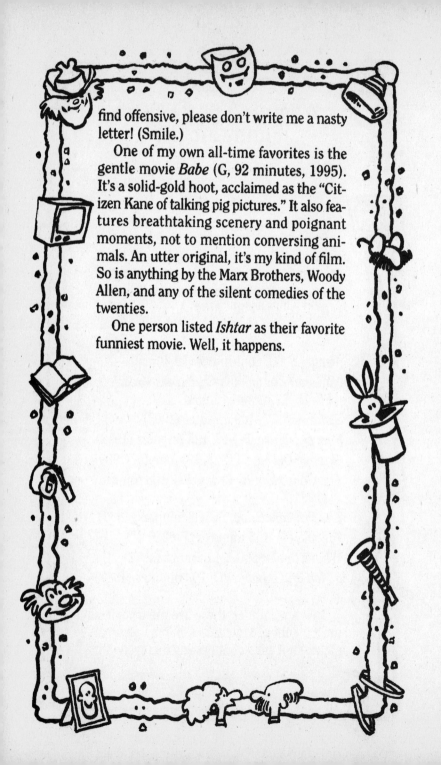

find offensive, please don't write me a nasty letter! (Smile.)

One of my own all-time favorites is the gentle movie *Babe* (G, 92 minutes, 1995). It's a solid-gold hoot, acclaimed as the "Citizen Kane of talking pig pictures." It also features breathtaking scenery and poignant moments, not to mention conversing animals. An utter original, it's my kind of film. So is anything by the Marx Brothers, Woody Allen, and any of the silent comedies of the twenties.

One person listed *Ishtar* as their favorite funniest movie. Well, it happens.

Chapter 7

The Frustrated Laugh: How to De-Tangle a Bad Humor Day

Everything is funny, as long as it is happening to somebody else.
—Will Rogers

We've looked at polite laughs, clueless laughs, nervous laughs, relieved laughs, and now—*grrr!*—the *frustrated laugh*, a cross between a growl and a grin.

Like Ishtar, it happens. You wake up on the wrong side of the bed, the wrong side of the room, the wrong end of the country, and no matter how much you try to laugh away your frustration, it rears its ugly head.

Bad humor days are hairy, and all the shampoo and cream rinse in the beauty-salon world won't solve the problem.

Whenever I'm tempted to grumble that I'm having a bad day, I remember the wise words of a friend: "There are no such things as bad days, only bad moments in good days."

The next time your whine-o-meter is pegged in the red zone, it's helpful to remember:

1. It's only a bad moment.
2. This, too, shall pass.
3. It's still a good day.

4.   Everything is funny eventually.

Bad (Hair) Days

Azriella, a speaking buddy of mine from Pennsylvania, was having a bad hair day. A real one. She asked her husband if he might give her hair a slight trim and spare her an expensive trip to the salon, saving the family some much-needed cash. He'd been cutting their children's hair for years, so he blithely said, "Sure."

With the first snip of the scissors, she realized that she and her husband had very different notions of what trim means. As Azriella describes it, "I wanted to scream as I felt the scissors press against my neck and saw my shoulder-length hair fall to the floor. But after that first snip, what good would screaming do? So I closed my eyes, took a deep breath, and waited for him to finish."

Finally, he snapped his scissors shut with a flourish and asked, "What do you think?"

In the mirror she saw a shocked woman wearing a brand-new pixie cut. She detangled her bad-humor day with a heroic turn of mind. "My first instinct was to scream or cry, but I quickly found the humor in it and said calmly, 'Well, dear, it's quite a bit shorter than I had in mind, so we'd better cut my bangs to match.'"

Then she complimented him on giving her a fabulous haircut.

(Never mind Dustin Hoffman. This woman gets the Oscar for Best Performance by a Wife Under Duress.)

Azriella admits the moral of the story is: Define *trim*. She is clearly a woman who values a great man over a bad haircut. Very smart.

A Hairy Story

I personally wouldn't let my dear Bill anywhere near my hair. The truth is, the woman I pay to hold the scissors sometimes gives me pause. Oh, there were a few days back in 1988 when I thought we'd really hit on something, but the rest of the time it's too long, too short, too curly, too flat, too red, too blonde, or decidedly too gray—though that last one is not my stylist's fault.

As for the cutting and styling itself, that's where I do depend on Carol. I've known her longer than I've known my husband. Our paths crossed in 1984, and I've faithfully sat in her chair ever since. When Carol switched salons, I followed her across town.

"Whither thou goest, I will go," I assured her.

Who wouldn't declare lifelong loyalty to someone who combines amateur therapy skills with the latest techniques in blunt cutting?

Carol listened patiently through my career and dating woes, nodding sympathetically as her scissors snipped away. Those were the perm years—natural color, unnatural curl. Then when hubby-to-be Bill came into my life, Carol and I dumped the perm in favor of longer locks to please my sweetie.

What is it with men and long hair?

Months later, it was Carol who styled the tresses of my wedding party, and Carol again who gave me a pedicure the week before my first child was slated to arrive, so I'd have fashionable toes in the delivery room.

Talk about a labor of love!

Our relationship isn't one-sided, either. I sang at Carol's wedding and rejoiced when she began taking college courses at night. We've laughed, cried, and compared notes on husbands, kids, and cleaning services. You can't simply walk away from that kind of dual commitment over something as frivolous as a few frizzy perms or doubtful dye jobs.

Besides, the mere thought of trying a new stylist gives me the willies. Make that will-he's. As in, "Will he understand about my sparse spots?" or "Will she know how to tame that strange cowlick in the back?" Someone else might do a better job, but then again, what if it's worse? What if my hair comes out five different lengths and three different colors?

Hey, it can happen. Carol once had to rescue a poor high school senior who'd dyed his hair purple to match his prom tux. He spent five hours (and untold dollars) in her chair while she corrected another stylist's nightmare-in-violet creation.

But he probably never darkened her chair again. Men are fickle when it comes to hair. Any five-dollar barber will do. The way my Bill sees it, why bother making an appointment with a pricey stylist when he can drop in Buck's Barber Shop unannounced, thumb through a few issues of *Field & Stream*, plunk down a ten, and leave with change and short hair?

"But what do you and Buck talk about?" I once asked him.

He wrinkled his brow in confusion. "I dunno. The weather? Reds baseball, maybe?" Bill sighed. "Look, the whole thing takes ten minutes, tops."

Aha! There's the difference. Women spend a minimum of forty-five minutes in a salon; two hours with color; three hours for a perm with a manicure. Toss in a facial or a wax job, and we're approaching half a day with our smocked sister.

We spend more money with them too. Lots more money. Bill was aghast the first time he saw a credit-card receipt from a visit with Carol. "Sixty dollars?!? You look the same as you did this morning. Can't you find someone less expensive?"

Less expensive, sure. But that's not the point. Carol and I are friends. Girl buddies. Partners in the fight against dark roots and stray chin hairs. She's seen me in no makeup. No clothes, for that matter, stretched out on a massage table wearing nothing but a towel and a smile.

Who could say sayonara to a soul sister like that?

One January, however, I came frighteningly close to committing hair-care infidelity. Just the memory of it makes my scalp itch. I was facing a photo session for a local magazine cover, and arrangements were made for Jacobson's to do my makeup and hair. After the cosmetician did a bang-up job on eyes, lips, and cheeks, it was time to put my thinning hair in the hands of a stranger named Steve.

Steve the Stylist rested his hands lightly on my shoulders, and my stomach tightened. I felt like a nervous teenager on a first date.

"Is there a particular way you'd like me to style your hair?"

Yes, I wanted to say. Carol's way! Instead, I gulped. "Nooo, just make me look ten pounds thinner and I'll be happy."

His graceful hands danced around my head, comb in one hand, industrial-strength hair spray in the other. I watched in amazement. I was getting thinner!

Gee, Carol never parted it like that. How did he do that lift-and-poof thing on the side? Fascinating.

Steve finally whipped off my plastic cape with a flourish. "There you are, Liz. What do you think?"

I think I'm in love. No, no, not with you, just your hands. Are you this good with scissors? Know your way around a bottle of peroxide? I realized the dangerous path my imagination was taking me down and mentally swatted away the little voices saying, "He's the one! He's the one! Leave Carol and cleave to Steve!"

When he slipped me his card and suggested I give him a call sometime, I stuffed it in my pocket, mumbled a red-faced "thank you," and hotfooted it for the door.

Whew! That was close. I'd resisted temptation, but barely. How could I even think of breaking up a friendship that was in its second decade, just for the thrill of a zippy new do? Sure, Steve might have some fresh ideas for my stale tresses, but what would I say when I saw Carol at the grocery store after being absent from her chair for six months and sporting a new color or cut? Even without a big red *A* on my chest, she would know: I'd been unfaithful.

I knew I should have tossed Steve's business card in the circular file, but I couldn't resist tucking it in my Rolodex, "just in case." In case Carol moved away or quit the business. Or was eaten by sharks. Otherwise, I would not defect to Steve. Would not, could not.

But my fingers kept flipping past his name. Hmm. Would Carol notice if I did one little color weave with Steve? Maybe a teensy trim, between real haircuts? If I timed it right, she'd never be the wiser. I reached for the phone and dialed Steve's salon.

The receptionist was sharp, cool, professional. Yes, Steve had an opening on Tuesday. A trim? Of course, no problem, 2:00 is fine. See you then, Mrs. Higgs.

I almost slammed the phone down. What was I thinking?

As the calendar marched toward Tuesday, I spent more time on my hair than usual, trying to convince myself to undo our risk-filled liaison. It's not that bad a cut, I told myself. In fact, it's a very good cut, or Steve couldn't have styled it so nicely.

Tuesday morning dawned gray and menacing. Cowardice leaped from my heart and into my fingers as I dialed the Other Salon's number and canceled my appointment, muttering a feeble excuse about my too-full schedule.

I waited for my racing heart to slow back down to normal and then hit the speed-dialing button that instantly put me in touch with my regular salon. My salon, Carol's salon. Home.

"A cut with Carol at 2:00 o'clock? No problem, Liz. See you then. Hug the kids for me."

Ahh. I hung up the phone in blessed relief, silently slipping Steve's card in the wastebasket. No more flirting with temptation; I'd stick with a place where everybody knows my name.

Especially Carol, the one woman who can (almost) guarantee me a good hair day.

Chapter 8

The Tickled Laugh: Tickling Permitted (Funny Bones Only, Please)

If you tickle us, do we not laugh?
—Shakespeare

It's not a polite laugh, nor clueless—since we know exactly what causes it—nor is it stimulated by nerves or relief or sheer frustration. It's the sound we make when we're tickled—the *tickled laugh.*

I don't get tickled pink, I get tickled beet red. When I was a kid, my brothers and sisters loved nothing better than twiddling their fingers in my most ticklish spots—behind my knees, under my elbows, on the soles of my feet—until I was lobster red and wheezing.

Don't you just love siblings? This is not what Paul meant when he wrote, "Yes, brother, let me have joy from you" (Philemon 20). Joy, yes, but not via tickling!

When I became a mother, I'm ashamed to admit that I, too, became a mad tickler. My children giggled so adorably, and their tootsies were so soft and cute. Surely it wasn't all that bad.

The problem is, they didn't laugh because it was funny, they laughed as a reflex action, even as their body jerked away as if under attack. Such uncontrollable laughter on their part— and very controllable twiddling on my part—is the problem with tickling.

It's a control issue.

I decided I'd rather have people laughing at me voluntarily, so the only thing I try to tickle now is someone's funny bone.

In my spare time, I tickle my own.

Sometimes we get tickled, not physically, but mentally. And that results in the tickled laugh.

Duck, Duck, Goose

We have a lovely lake next door that belongs to our neighbors (seems only fair—it's on their land), but which we also enjoy through the window. Canada geese come whooshing out of the sky in season, and a whole family of ducks makes its home there as well. One spring we watched a mother mallard lead her ducklings along our driveway, under the fence, and over to the lake. Charming.

Then a few days later, Bill called me over to a spot in the grass, finger to his lips. "Shh! Come see," he whispered.

I peered down at the small hole in the ground, where a tiny baby animal was obviously hiding. All I could see was a soft, downy brown. "Ohh!" I gasped softly, pointing. "Duck!"

Bill's eyebrows shot up into his forehead. "A what?"

At that moment, a large, brown mother rabbit hopped over, looking agitated.

Was she unhappy because I was near her baby, or because I falsely accused it of being fowl-y rather than furry?

We tiptoed away, and as soon as it seemed safe, exploded with laughter. Bill, who almost never laughs out loud, was bent over.

He could only say one thing. "Duck?! Duck!?"

Now whenever either one of us identifies something incorrectly, we just shrug and say, "Duck." And get tickled all over again.

What a Cutup!

Kathleen managed to tickle her funny bone quite by accident while sitting in an elegant hotel lobby in downtown Seattle and waiting for her husband to come out of a seminar. The magazine article she was reading included a photo of an X ray of a man's throat. It seemed he had swallowed a table knife while eating peas.

Suddenly, the very idea of such a ludicrous thing happening washed over Kathleen and she got tickled. "It struck me so funny, I hugged the walls to keep upright while I found my way outside, passing a lobby filled with people staring at me like, 'That woman has lost it!'"

Sitting outside on the front steps in her pretty spring dress, Kathleen laughed hysterically for the next twenty minutes. Meanwhile, her husband heard about the crazy woman outside, and when he realized it was his wife, he simply walked past her. Once she could compose herself enough to walk a straight line, she followed him—at a safe distance—to their car.

Bless her heart, the woman couldn't help herself. She literally had no control. Just like the child getting tickled physically, she got tickled mentally, with the same results: *Haa!*

This happens occasionally among audience members. I'll see a person bending over, red faced, obviously having trouble breathing, and even as I continue telling some tale, I keep an anxious eye on her. What is going on? Is she okay?

Then my eyes widen. Oh, no. The woman next to her is doing the same thing. It's contagious, and it's headed this direction! One by one, people bend over, lean back, fall sideways, turn red, and gasp for breath.

Sneezing and hiccuping are not contagious. Yawning and laughing are.

I've seen some individuals go off the deep end and not be able to get back. Everyone around them begins to draw away, fearing the contagion. Try as they might, though, they can't pull themselves together. Their loud whooping eases up for a breathless moment, then off they go again.

Their friends shrug their shoulders. "She's not usually like this," they mouth carefully.

The rest of the audience stares at me. Can't you do something about this?

Gee, do I have to? If I was the one who brought all this on, I love it. In truth, it was their own fearfully and wonderfully-made mind that went off on its own tangent. That's why they got tickled, never to return. I was merely a mirror, allowing them to discover something funny inside themselves.

When the tickle takeover happens to me, I never see it coming. Some lightly amusing thing happens, and out comes this "Harrr!"

We're talking waaay past hoot.

I start slapping the table, the dashboard, whatever is handy and can withstand my pounding. No sooner do I reign it in than it washes over me again like the waves at Ocean City, knocking me off balance.

Bill just shakes his head. The kids love it, of course.

Northern Disclosure

Several years ago, when Matthew and Lillian were six and four, they saw me at my all-time silliest. We went on a moose-hunting trip to Alaska. No, not that kind of hunting, with guns and trophies and such. This was an "Oh, look! A moose!" sort of hunt as we traveled the highway between Anchorage and Talkeetna.

Moose-viewing was the main selling point that helped our kids sit still on the plane for some dozen hours. The minute we took off in our rental car, we kept our eyes glued to the woods along the roadside, slowing down at the moosiest looking spots, certain we'd spot one any minute. Sadly, day one came and went without a single sighting.

Dinner that evening at the Klondike Café featured salmon (what else?) for Mom and Dad, burgers for the kids. When I suggested they try the reindeer, four-year-old Lillian's eyes teared up at the very idea of serving Donner and Blitzen with ketchup. Bill then spotted moose on the menu, but Matthew just rolled his eyes.

"Dad, we'd like to see a live moose, not a cooked one."

By our last day, we were in major moose-hunting mode, desperate to see one of Alaska's most famous citizens. Pointing our rental car toward the airport, we were coming up on a busy intersection when, without warning, a huge moose—A MOOSE!—came crashing out of the bushes.

She bolted across the four-lane road, inches away from becoming our hood ornament. We got a bird's-eye—make that moose's-eye—view of very long legs in motion, a hump behind her head just like in the pictures, no antlers (she-moose don't have 'em) and more body than head, with more legs than anything else.

Our only moose, in downtown Anchorage, of all places!

No one honked, no one braked, no one seemed the least bit surprised.

But those drivers were Alaskans. We were tourists. We were in hysterics. I was laughing so hard I had to lay my head on the steering wheel to catch my breath as our celebrity Alaskan cow disappeared into the nearby woods.

Raining Cats (Not Dogs)

Another animal altogether managed to elude Janis from California, despite her most valiant efforts.

Janis's aging, mellow marmalade feline, Francis, was being repeatedly harrassed by the neighbor's nasty cat, Pepper. The bully cat's owners were not too concerned, but Janis's vet bills were rising.

She didn't want to hurt Pepper, of course, only scare him away from their yard, so she decided a Bazooka Liquidator was the answer. We're talking one of those enormous water guns that squirts fifty feet. Janis explains, "I stomped into Toy World, pointed to the display of water guns behind the cash register, and announced, 'I need a gun—a *big* one!'"

The young woman behind the counter looked concerned. "Wouldn't you like to go home and discuss this with your husband?" she asked, but Janis assured her that her husband approved the weapon purchase.

Every time Janis saw Pepper in her yard, she ran out and blasted him with water, but he always got away. One morning, hearing some noise in the yard, Janis grabbed her Bazooka and charged out the back door, firing. "I'd forgotten this was the morning the mow-and-blow guys came" she confessed. A thoroughly terrified gardener narrowly escaped the Bazooka's furious flood.

He wasn't tickled about it, but Janis was.

The good news is, Pepper and his family moved away. The bad news is, a new family moved in with three cats. Stay tuned.

Slip Sliding Away, Part One

When it comes to getting tickled, nothing makes me laugh harder than physical comedy. No words, no story line, just a great sight gag or pratfall, the kind where nothing gets hurt but your dignity. Not the Three Stooges. That's a guy thing. We're talking Chevy Chase or *Airplane!*

Or Karla on skis.

"I'd been taking lessons on the beginning slope," Karla says, "and I got to where I wasn't falling too much. Then I decided to go down The Big Hill."

When she got up to the top, she had second thoughts, but no choice. "I couldn't stay up there forever, so I started down. Everything I'd learned disappeared from my mind. I yelled, 'Get out of the way! Get out of the way!' as I went straight down the hill. At the bottom was the lodge with a fence in front of it. Somehow, I dodged the fence and ran smack into the side of the building."

When Karla hobbled inside a few minutes later, she found her twin sister rolling on the floor.

"What is so funny?" Karla asked.

Holding her sides, tears running down her face, her sister gasped, "You missed it. Some idiot just ran into the lodge!"

Slip Sliding Away, Part Two

It was summer, not winter, and it was an inner tube, not a pair of skis, but the end result (pun intended) was much the same. One hot day I got really brave, put on a bathing suit (a navy-blue, no-nonsense, industrial-strength number), and went with Bill and the kids to a water park, the kind with wave pools and huge slides. One of the rides, as it were, was a water slide that twisted and turned from a dizzying height to a splash pool at the bottom.

You rode the slide in a huge inner tube by draping your arms over one side and your legs over the other and parking your bottom in the doughnut hole, so to speak. Easy enough for a young, agile mom, perhaps, but this fortysomething mother doesn't bend as well as she used to, and the rubber inner tube was less than cooperative.

Even with the hunky lifeguard-type helping me, I couldn't seem to get situated. The tube scooted one way, I scooted the other. Frustration quickly gave way to laughter, and then I was really in trouble. As you know only too well, when you start laughing, your muscles relax. Coordination is a thing of the past. The water flowing around the tube sent it spinning in a circle, which made me dizzy and tickled me even further.

My arms were hanging on to the soft, slippery inner tube for dear life, my long legs were sticking straight up in the air, and my ample bottom was parked deep in the doughnut hole, such that I was folded up tight as a card table and couldn't breathe.

But boy, could I laugh.

I was whooping in near hysteria as my family waited in line, pretending they had no connection to the wild woman in the navy-blue suit. The lifeguard gave my inner tube a shove, and down the slide I went, tossing caution and dignity to the winds. Gales of laughter followed me as I plunged sixty miles per hour down to the pool below

Ker-*splash!*

I hit that landing pool with such force that my own bottom went straight to the pool bottom and the inner tube shot up in the air some fifty feet, according to dozens of wide-eyed spectators. The lifeguard, who'd been listening to this traveling circus as it careened down the slide, now watched in horror as a large, laughing navy-blue woman disappeared beneath the foamy surface of the water.

"Are you okay, ma'am?" he hollered, grabbing my arm to pull me up for air.

I was still laughing, though it sounded more like gurgling. "I'm fine," I assured him, trying to get my breath. "I just got tickled at the top and couldn't stop."

"You did what?"

Another *haawww!* exploded from my lips. "Tickled," I gasped, "I got—oh, never mind. Here come the rest of my family."

Three more laughing Higgses hit the water. They looked tickled too.

"Mom, let's do it again!"

Sorry, one tickle a day is all I can handle.

Chapter 9

The Amused Laugh: Keep Your Wit About You

We're all pretty much alike when we get out of town.
—*Kin Hubbard*

Finally, the seventh reason—the real reason—we laugh is because something is genuinely funny. These are the best laughs, the heartiest chuckles, the ones that catch us by surprise.

Laughter is not a cerebral decision. No one looks at their watch with a dour face and says, "I think I'll laugh in thirteen seconds." Laughter isn't something you choose to do or not do, unless you've become adept at stuffing every other emotion as well.

The *amused laugh* travels the short distance from brain to mouth and, propelled by the diaphragm, explodes through the lips, bringing a smile not only to the face of the laugher but usually to the faces of all within earshot as well.

When I tell audiences, readers, and friends, "You gotta add more laughter to your life," they shake their heads.

"You just don't understand, Liz. I don't have your sense of humor."

Lucky you.

"You don't need to be funny," I assure them gently. "You need merely to appreciate the humor that's all around you."

"But I don't have time."

No time for laughter?

Mary from Kentucky admits as much. "I like to laugh but am too busy sometimes to find the humor in things."

What about popping a good clean comedy in the VCR tonight?

"I don't have time to rent a funny video," people whine. "Even if I did, I don't have time to watch it."

I've been there, haven't you? Rented a funny video on a Friday after work, with the best intentions of giving myself a humor break. When Sunday night rolled around, the tape was due back at the store by 8:00, so at 7:50 I desperately try to watch ten minutes of the movie to justify the $2.99 I paid to rent it.

Silly me.

You really don't have to buy or even rent humor, when God has graciously planted it all around you. "Seeing the silly side makes life fun," declares Annette from South Carolina.

Funny stuff is everywhere, if you know where to look. Out your car window, for instance. You can add lots of healthy humor to your life merely by slowing down to the speed limit (especially if your state is like Kentucky, where the speed limits are just a suggestion). Tighten your seat belt to be safe, then keep one eye on the amusing scenery along the road.

And do drive carefully. Carol from Alabama picked up her husband for a lunch date and got behind every awful driver on the road. She was ranting and raving about one driver's inability to use a turn signal or another one's decision to stop in the middle of the highway for no apparent reason.

Finally, she fumed, "You know, if I ever have a stroke, it will be while I'm driving."

Her husband didn't miss a beat. "Honey," he said, "if *I* ever have a stroke, it will be while you're driving!"

Sign Language

If you're ready to include more amusement in your laugh life, the first place to look are those roadside signs.

Lori from Indiana saw a sign posted outside a row of stores and offices shared by an OB/GYN and a carpet shop. It's not clear which one put the sign out front that boasted FREE DELIVERY.

A used car lot in Racine, Wisconsin, featured a sign that gave Betty a good laugh: WE SELL NO CARS ON SUNDAY AND PRECIOUS FEW DURING THE WEEK.

Cindy's friend Steve saw a sign in Montana: VETERINARIAN/TAXIDERMIST—EITHER WAY, YOU GET YOUR DOG BACK.

Judi from Georgia got a giggle when she saw a sign displayed at the gate of the Atlanta Open Golf Tournament that said, GOLFERS' WIVES—NO DOGS ALLOWED.

Well, the very idea.

Some signs strike an ominous note, like the one we saw in Alaska that hinted of the long, dark winter that was only weeks away: HAVE YOU HAD YOUR BATTERY CHECKED? THE NIGHT IS COMING.

Around Christmas time, a Hoosier woman spotted a sign that offered BALD CHRISTMAS TREES. (Just a trunk with bare branches, do you suppose?) I saw a similar sign posted at a booksellers convention that announced TODAY AT 3:00, MEET YOUR FAVORITE BALD EAGLE PAINTER.

Bless his heart—and his shiny head.

Here's a cryptic pair of signs found on a Florida highway. The first sign said, PANTHER CROSSING, NEXT 11 MILES. Then three miles later, the second sign read, PICNIC AREA, 6 MILES.

Who's having the picnic—people or panthers?

Speaking of ferocious animals, a friend noted a sign that cautioned FORGET DOG—BEWARE OF OWNER.

And here's a frightening "Father's Day Special" offered by a local restaurant: ADULTS $6.95/CHILDREN $4.95—SERVED HOT TODAY FROM 11:00 A.M. TO 10:00 P.M.

But where was the sign—any sign—when Alice needed one?

Crusin' for Amusin'

Alice from Texas moved to the small town of Andrews and decided to explore her new surroundings. She ventured out, soon became disoriented about which direction she was driving, and found herself turning onto a small country road that was only wide enough for one car.

As Alice tells it, "Then I realized I was on the golf-cart path of the local country club!" Not wanting to ruin their manicured fairways and greens, she quickly proceeded past the clubhouse (where onlookers were doing double and triple takes) and on up to the northern end, trying to find a short escape route.

Alice continues, "Finally finding a wide paved area, I turned off, only to find I was now on the airport runway."

It didn't take her long to find her way back into town from that popular spot. Shortly thereafter a bar gate with a large sign appeared at Alice's new entrance: NO TRESPASSING.

Brenda from Florida was taking the shuttle from La Guardia Airport to the Marriott and passed several signs along the road that warned CAUTION: LOW FLYING AIRCRAFT.

"I wasn't quite sure what we were supposed to do," Brenda admits. "Duck our heads? Veer off the road when a plane was approaching?"

Then there's the one I've spotted on my visits to San Diego, and Linda from Missouri saw it too. On Route 5 near downtown is this sign that gives one pause: CRUISE SHIPS—USE HOTEL EXIT. Just for the record, I've not been passed on the San Diego freeway by a cruise ship yet, but if it happens I'll try to act natural.

And, beware when you are traveling in the suburbs of Oklahoma City, where a sign warns DANGEROUS PEDESTRIAN INTERSECTION.

Finding humor in print is simple enough. Just look in the classified ads, which is where the following unintentional laugh lines were found:

- Dog for sale—eats anything and is fond of children.
- Tired of cleaning yourself? Let me do it.
- Now is your chance to have your ears pierced and get an extra pair to take home too.

Here's an unusual excerpt from a church bulletin, inviting members to the Beginning Again Seminar:

Help for the Formally Married.

Sherry caught this blooper in her own Sunday bulletin:

Hearing assistance devices are available. If you need one, please an usher.

Travel-Size Humor

Gayle was spending a rare night away from home, attending an educational conference. "It was about one in the morning and we girls had just finished our slumber-party talk in my hotel room. I slipped into my navy silk nightshirt, brushed my teeth, and decided to tidy up my room, including disposing of my room-service tray."

Those of us who travel often may see what's coming next.

"I opened my door and gently lowered the tray to the hall floor when I heard the heavy thud of the room door closing behind me. I was now stranded in the hotel hallway in my nightgown. I didn't have the nerve to knock on a neighbor's door at 1:00 A.M., so instead I leaned over the lobby railing of this grand hotel and hollered, 'Is anyone down there?'"

A bewildered bellhop looked up, and Gayle explained her predicament. He promised to send someone up, and after what seemed like an eternity, the manager arrived. As he opened the door he merely smiled and said, "Well, lady, at least you had some clothes on."

Gayle wanted to know, "Liz, with all your travels, has this ever happened to you?"

Not yet, but I've come v-e-r-y close. I usually stand safely inside my room and push the tray of dishes out into the hallway with my big toe. Late one night, garbed in the silliest excuse for pajamas you've ever seen, I was carefully guiding the room-service tray inch by inch across the threshold of my door, trying my best not to knock over the stack of dishes.

So focused was I on moving this tray, I never looked up until it was safely clear of my doorway. My gaze landed on half a dozen couples returning to their rooms, dressed to the nines from a party, staring at big Liz in her too-short, too-tight Daffy Duck pajamas and nothing else, playing footsie with a tray.

Gayle, next time, let's leave the dishes in the room.

Traveling literally keeps you on your toes, and since you're more aware of your unfamiliar surroundings, you often see humor that might escape your notice at home.

One major hotel chain has a little tent sign on the nightstand with this encouraging invitation: PLEASE CALL THE FRONT DESK IF YOU LEFT ANYTHING AT HOME.

I eye the phone, wondering if I dare press 0 and do as they've requested—"Yes, this is Room 502, and I left behind my husband, two children, one cat, a couple of couches, a fake eucalyptus tree . . ."

Of course, we know what such signs really mean, but humor comes from meaning one thing and saying altogether another.

Another little sign appeared on the desk: PLEASE DO NOT IRON ON THE FURNITURE. Golly, it didn't even look wrinkled. If it did, I certainly wouldn't feel compelled to iron it, would you?

In the pool area of the hotel, the sign clearly stated, NO WET SUITS. Yes, yes, we know what they mean, but it's hard to imagine going swimming without getting your suit wet.

In the bathroom of a rural hotel room were some unusual signs: DO NOT PLACE CIGARETTES ON TUB. Again, it's obvious what they were getting at—don't sit in the tub with a lighted cigarette, then lay it down on the edge and ruin the surface—but the temptation was too strong for me.

Deciding it was worth the two-dollar investment, I visited the vending machine down the hall and bought a pack of Marlboros. I didn't light them, of course, but instead stood all twenty of them on their filtered ends, marching around the edge of the tub.

Then I waited till the maid showed up.

Another surprise waited for me when I climbed in this same bathtub and saw the sign above the shower nozzle: PLACE CURTAIN IN TUB. Good heavens, what a lot of trouble. With a sigh, I took down the drapes and stretched them out in the tub, hoping I'd managed this task to their liking.

Honestly, you'd think they'd have their curtains professionally cleaned.

Another hotel apparently wearied of people stealing all the little bars of soap, and so put two soap dispensers in the shower instead. Fine, but which was which? I didn't need deodorant soap on my face, thank you very much. My lips almost never sweat.

It was a moot point, since these soap dispensers were like every dispenser you've ever seen in a public place—empty.

PART THREE

Laughing Moments

Humor is a universal tool for relating to others. Helen from Glasgow, Scotland, who insists the funniest woman she knows is "my mum!" wrote, "A male friend tried to chat up a girl who wasn't too keen. He invited her for dinner on Friday night, to which she replied, 'I'm not going to be hungry on Friday night!'"

I hope the chap had a sense of humor. When it comes to relationships, it's a must-have component for compatibility. Humor breaks the ice, builds rapport, and heals hurt feelings. As Dana from Ohio sees it, "Humor is like a credit card: Never leave home without it."

Chapter 10

Humor and Marriage: Are You Married to a Funny-Baked Ham?

> Groucho: *Are you married?*
> Guest: *No, I'm separated.*
> Groucho: *Maybe you've been using the wrong kind of glue.*
> —Groucho Marx on You Bet Your Life

This chapter title assumes you have a Honey-Baked Ham store in your neck of the woods, though since I'm cooking impaired, anything I pull out of the oven will be "funny-baked."

My wonderful Bill, first and only husband of a dozen years, is definitely sweet as honey and anything but half-baked. But he is a ham radio operator and he is funny, as in ha-ha funny. Those who only see his quiet side never believe me, but it's true: Bill is much funnier than I am. His one-liners are a work of art; his spin on life is clever beyond measure. Blessed woman that I am, I get to bask in his good-natured humor every day of my life.

Considering how long I looked for my Prince Charming, it's only fair that I found a prince after such a l-o-n-g line of toads. (Say, if you meet a toad sitting on a barstool, would that make it a *toadstool*?)

When you're seventeen years young, men and marriage are a thrilling, frightening prospect in the distant future. Oh, but we planned, we prepared, we made lists of all the qualities our mate-for-life was required to have before we'd even give him a second glance. At seventeen, the list was very long indeed. It filled a legal pad, which we happily covered with ink during study hall.

Everything matters at seventeen.

When I reached twenty-one, still single, I crossed a few things off my long list. For starters, my dream man no longer needed long, curly eyelashes. I could skip that. He didn't have to drive a Camaro, either. A Nova would do. A Pinto, even.

At twenty-five, I went back to my list and ripped off the bottom half. Let's just stick with the core stuff, I told myself.

By thirty I was working with a Post-it note. By thirty-two I had one word left—*breathing*.

Bill breathes well. He also has everything I had on my long list, except hair. Who cares about such things when you're thirtysomething? I love his slippery scalp and the humorous outlook on life that lives under it.

One of the secrets to a happy marriage, we think, is remembering the Source of our joy, which isn't each other. The Source of our joy is the Lord. Yes, we share tons of joyous moments, but we don't expect, let alone demand, joy from our partner. Lot of pressure there. Instead, we look to the same Source, and find the Lord ever available.

In Your presence is fullness of joy;
At Your right hand are pleasures forevermore. (Psalm 16:11)

Happily Ever Laughter

Bill and I are not only partners in life and in parenting, we're also partners in business. June from Pennsylvania was in business with her hubby, too, but before they were married; in fact, before they were even dating. Andy still lived with his parents in Brooklyn but didn't want any of the women he dated to know that, so he gave them June's phone number, which doubled as their business phone.

Hmm, not very romantic. Yet.

After a year of taking messages for him, June was painting a garage floor side by side with Andy one day when she blurted out, "We see each other every day anyway, we might as well get married."

He said okay, and the rest is history! June and Andy celebrated ten years of wedded bliss on October 17, 1997, with four children—ages seven, five, four, and two. Concerning her unusual proposal, June quipped, "Is this biblical? Well, I think God had it planned all along!"

Cindy from Georgia is a happily married woman—twenty-two years and counting. The receptionist at the school where she teaches wants to keep it that way. When the school psychologist called to discuss a student they were evaluating together, he asked, "Is Cindy available?" to which the witty receptionist responded, "Certainly not! She's married."

Snail Male

Dan and Mary were in the early days of courting when he took her to a romantic seacoast spot to spend a warm spring afternoon. They watched the tide go in and out and tried to impress one another with their confidence, cleverness, and charm.

Dan gallantly held her hand as they gingerly stepped from one slippery rock to the next and soon found themselves quite a distance out from shore. Since they'd been gazing into each other's eyes, they'd neglected to notice that they'd run out of rocks and were actually stepping on snails, thousands of snails!

Mary confesses, "There isn't much that shakes me, but when I recognized the crunch underfoot to be newly deceased snails, and all I could see for what seemed like miles was a sea of live snails coming at me, I froze in absolute terror. There I stood, eyes filled with tears, laughing hysterically one minute, whimpering the next, silently begging myself to not lose my composure or ask Dan for help."

Dan is four inches shorter than Mary and of slighter build, so carrying her to safety was not an option. The tide was returning and their choices were limited, so brave Dan confidently grabbed her hand [the hero's theme rises to crescendo here] and with one decisive swoop he began kicking the snails out of her way so she could step on solid, sandy ground while he lovingly encouraged her. "Hold on, you can do it, I'll get you to safety."

In a good romance novel, the story would end with them serving escargot at their wedding reception, but I'll settle for "they lived happily ever after." And they have.

Ronda from New Mexico had a wedding to remember. The bride and groom were dressed in turn-of-the-century costumes complete with top hat, parasol, and bustle dress "that brought snickers and all-out guffaws from family and friends." When the moment came to share their own words of love and commitment, the groom pulled his notes from his pocket and shook out a l-o-n-g list that rolled down the aisle of the church.

Well, why not include humor during your wedding ceremony? The Lord knows you'll need it on your honeymoon. "The quality I love the most about my husband is his dry wit," says Cathy from Oklahoma. "It's made hard times much more bearable."

Rain Falling on Cedars

Regina started dating Ted in April, and by Christmas she was a little depressed about missing her family and their traditions. One of those customs was a cedar Christmas tree, which Ted from the East Coast had never heard of.

On his way home from work one day in December he spotted a grove of cedar trees around an abandoned home. Perfect! They waited until dark, got their flashlights, and drove forty-five minutes back to the grove of trees.

Regina points out, "It was much darker and scarier at night, especially when the wind blew and made strange sounds." They decided to take only the top half of a tree, but it still took Ted a full hour to get the treetop off. Hiding from all the car lights slowed things down, too, and then it started to rain. When they dragged the treetop to his car, they realized the key to the trunk was missing.

They left the tree—grumbling all the way, we're certain—and returned the next night with a bigger car. Regina and Ted got scratched and bruised loading the cedar tree in the trunk, and again when it fell out on the way home. Finally they maneuvered the tree up a tricky staircase and dragged it into her apartment.

Ta-da! and Merry Christmas, right?

Not quite.

They placed the tree in a new, expensive stand and faced the awful truth. As Regina put it, "It was the ugliest, skinniest Charlie Brown tree you ever saw. We laughed until we cried."

In Silliness and in Health

Marriage is more manageable with humor. Laughing relationships last longer, and couples who cut up create ties that bind for a lifetime. Sandy from Pennsylvania sees it this way: "After all these years of marriage, there's a sense of 'this-oughta-be-good!' in our approach to each other's idiosyncrasies. Laughter is just another way of saying I love you."

Cathy was sitting on the couch when she heard the dryer go off. She knew the clothes couldn't be dry yet, so since her husband, John, was in the kitchen, she called out to him, "Honey, please turn on the dryer, would you?"

Soon she overheard him saying: "Ooh, Ba-by, I love you so much. You're so beautiful. I love your lint trap."

"What on earth are you doing?" Cathy called out.

"Turning on the dryer."

First Comes Love, Then Comes Marriage, Then . . .

Bill from New Jersey confesses, "I hate hospitals. In fact, when my wife, Jan, was expecting our first child, I got sick just taking the tour of the maternity floor. The very thought of going into the labor room was enough to send me over the edge."

The night Jan went into labor, Bill sat in the waiting room anticipating the moment when he would assume the role of coach. When the nurse came with his hospital attire, she instructed him to go through the double doors and enter the first room on his left.

Bill says, "I was a wreck but was determined I could do this. I marched through the doors and entered the room, only to find my bride, legs draped in a sheet, already in the stirrups. I lovingly reached over, rested my hand on her leg, took a deep breath, and peered over the sheet—it wasn't Jan! I'd turned to the right instead of the left."

The humiliation continued when later that week at the special couples' dinner provided by the hospital, Bill sat next to the same woman and her husband. A year later, standing behind the counter of his bookstore, waiting on customers, Bill watched with dismay as this woman approached the counter and smiled. "Haven't we met someplace before?"

As some anonymous soul wisely said, "A husband is one who stands by you in troubles you wouldn't have had if you hadn't married him."

Not-So-Silent Night

This wasn't Dana's hubby's fault, but he was there when it all happened.

Dana fell asleep dreaming and woke up screaming, certain that a man had broken into their hotel room. She says, "As my dream became more intense, I began stirring in my sleep. When my sensitive husband lovingly embraced me, I thought I was being attacked by the man in my dream and started fighting for my life."

Suddenly she heard a loud crash and woke up. "My heart was racing out of control, and I shouted out my husband's name. A voice from across the room said, 'I'm over here.'"

In her nightmarish panic, she'd launched her husband out of bed and sent the nightstand lamp flying as well. Dana says, "The people at the Sheraton were very nice when my husband explained about the broken lamp."

It wasn't a good night for Pat from Missouri either. Falling into bed exhausted, she'd no sooner slipped into a deep sleep when "a loud thunderous noise woke me, and I bolted upright. It took me a moment before I realized the noise was my husband snoring. I gently nudged him and he stopped so I dropped off to sleep again. This time the noise was much louder, and there was no doubt of its source. I pushed him on his side, sure that would do the trick."

Seconds later, she was awakened to the loudest snoring she'd ever heard. "I woke him up and insisted that he stop snoring. He kindly obliged and then drifted back to sleep. But within seconds of my sleep the noise started up again. How could he snore so loud?"

It was only then that the shocking realization hit her: *She* was the one snoring, not her husband. "I was so embarrassed. Then I started laughing out loud because of the wonderful joke I'd played on myself. I couldn't stand to have all this joy without sharing it, so I woke up my husband for the fourth time and shared the news with him."

Pat insists she snores only when she has a cold. Her husband isn't talking. Or snoring.

Lord, Give Me Strength and a Good Sense of Direction

Because our driveway stretches a l-o-n-g 600 feet from door to street, my hubby, Bill, avoided paving our driveway for two years, hoping the price of asphalt would suddenly plummet to an all-time low. But when yet another summer downpour washed away the gravel that masqueraded as our driveway, frugal Bill succumbed to the inevitable—a visit from Blacktop Man.

The estimate was ugly. Bill felt too faint even to write the check, so I filled in all the zeros. With payment now assured, half a dozen gruff and grimy men began pouring tar and pebbles down the length of our drive, which suddenly appeared to stretch for six or seven miles from house to mailbox.

To get our cars out of the asphalt zone, we parked them in a ditch at the end of the lane, figuring, Hey, we're out in the country. No one will mind.

They minded.

"Don't leave those cars here overnight!" said the police.

"But where else can we park them?" we whined.

"On a side street with a curb." They seemed very firm on this point, so while asphalt rained down on our gravel drive, Bill prowled the neighborhood for unsuspecting side streets until he stumbled on a distant subdivision with ample parking. The hike back home took nearly half an hour, but the car was safely curbside and was no longer in danger of being arrested for vagrancy.

Meanwhile, my own car and I had vacated the ditch and headed downtown for a dinner meeting. Returning home long after sunset, I absentmindedly turned into our freshly-paved driveway—horrors!—before yellow sawhorses screamed WARNING: FRESH BLACKTOP.

Hastily backing out, I eased down the street. Where had Bill told me to park? I drove around in squares (who drives around in circles?), wishing I'd brought my cell phone, until I spotted Bill's car and parked behind it, relieved to clear the first hurdle of the evening. Now came the tricky part—finding our house in the dark. On foot.

The night was mild, a blessing since I'd forgotten a coat, but the moonless sky was inky black. Up and down the street, lights glowing behind curtains made me long for our own cozy house somewhere out there in the darkness. My high heels, designed only for looking smashing while seated, now made their painful, precarious presence known. "Ouch!" I grumbled under my breath, teeter-tottering down the rough pavement.

That's when I saw it: There, between two houses, beyond a cornfield, was the familiar outline of our barn. As the crow flies, I wasn't far from home after all.

Too bad I wasn't a crow.

Instead, I was a determined woman in horrible shoes bent on finding the shortest distance between two points. I marched up the nearest driveway, paying no attention to the child staring out the window and pointing at me, and started across the backyard.

A vague discomfort settled over me. *Was this trespassing?* I wondered, gingerly stepping around flower beds and garden tools. Is the penalty for this worse than leaving your car in a ditch?

Grateful that tall fences weren't popular in our end of the county, I crossed over to the next yard when suddenly from a corner of the darkness came a loud *grrrgghhh*. An invisible dog was guarding his territory, no doubt. It sounded like a very large breed with not-so-invisible teeth.

"Nice doggie," I said, not meaning a word of it. More growling. High-heeled or not, I hustled into the next yard and prayed I wouldn't find another four-legged security guard.

No such luck. This one was a howler. Long, mournful, wolfy whines filled the air as a screen door banged open. "Who is it?" a male voice demanded to know.

"I'm Liz," I called back, feeling foolish and sounding like Dorothy from Kansas. "I live over there," I added, waving in the general direction of our barn, still far off in the distance. "We, uh, we had our driveway paved."

Even the canine howling stopped with that one.

"You what?" The man in the doorway was trying to sound very authoritative, but the lurking smile in his voice gave him away.

I sighed, desperation beginning to set in. "I had to park my car along your curb because I couldn't park in my own driveway." What kind of an explanation was that? Thank goodness it was enough for him.

"No problem, ma'am, just watch out for T-Bone there. He doesn't cotton to strangers."

I gave T-Bone a wide berth and pressed on through the darkness until a slatted wooden fence presented a momentary obstacle. I fumbled along for a latch for a gate. When the rusty hinges groaned in the night like a scene from a grade-B horror flick, I let loose a nervous giggle. *Get a grip, Liz.*

Our barn now beckoned like an oasis across the harvested cornfield. *This should be easy enough to cross.* Silly me. The field was a land mine of holes, rocks, and cornstalks. My shoes were soon up to their insteps in loamy earth. I resorted to marching along like a four year old at the beach, trying not to sink in any deeper lest I end up in China.

Only a hundred yards or so stretched between me and our dear, dilapidated barn. One more fence and I was home free. A hasty inspection brought bad news: The fencing was wire and had no gate. Launching my larger-than-average body over sharp metal seemed foolish, even dangerous, but launch it I would.

I found a discarded wooden crate, prayed it would hold me, and climbed on. The absence of splintering sounds buoyed my confidence. Guessing the distance and hoping for a soft landing, I took a deep breath and leaped over the fence, high heels in hand.

Thwommpp.

It was a soft landing, all right. Too soft. Squishy, even. I was soon up to my knees in whatever it was. Not manure, thank goodness, but not dirt, either. Too soft for leaves, too warm for sand. *Oh, my, it couldn't be . . .*

I had landed in our neighbor's compost heap. It had to be four feet deep and ten feet wide. Getting out was going to be problematic at best. One wrong move and I could tumble face first into the muck. Yuck.

"Help!" I whispered faintly to no one in particular. My arms were the only thing I could move safely, so I flapped them up and down like a big chicken, hoping someone, anyone, might happen by and rescue me. "Help, help," I said again with less enthusiasm. Who was I kidding? Nobody visits their compost heap in the dark. *Except . . .*

No! I refused to think about the various critters that probably spent many a happy night in a compost heap. I was in the midst of devising the best route of escape from my compost prison when, out of the corner of my eye, I spied a light bobbing along in my direction. Just a few feet off the ground and seemingly attached to nothing, it slowly grew brighter, weaving along an eerie path of its own making, hovering in the night, like a . . .like a . . .

"Aahhh!" The scream wasn't a planned thing, it just happened. "Aahhh!" I screamed again before my throat tightened completely. Suddenly the light was moving toward me and picking up speed. It seemed to be part of something bigger, something with legs.

The legs had a voice. "Liz? Are you okay?"

I almost dropped seat first into the compost. Bill, my beloved Bill, had come to rescue me. "Oh, honey, help me out," I stammered, feeling weepy and light-headed with relief.

Bill put down his big flashlight, practically lifted me out of the mountain of compost—no easy feat—and brushed the worst of it off my legs.

"How did you hear me way out here?" My voice was shaking like a woman who'd just had a close encounter with an alien.

"I didn't hear you, Liz." He tracked down his flashlight and began moving toward the barn. "I saw your car pass by the end of our driveway thirty minutes ago and knew you should've been home by now." Even in the darkness, I could see his grin. "I figured you'd try to find a shortcut."

"Yeah, well, I found one all right." I started to follow him across the grass and realized I was in my stocking feet. "I'll take my shoes now, honey."

"Uh, your what?"

"My heels. Don't you have them?"

We both turned back and gazed at the compost heap, now a shapeless mountain in the darkness.

I found my voice first. "Look, I never liked those shoes. Mister Gardening Guru is welcome to them. How long does it take patent leather to decompose anyway?"

Hardly noticing the sticks and stones tearing up my pantyhose as I tiptoed toward the house, I sent up a silent prayer of thanks for my ever-watchful mate and recalled the verse from Ecclesiastes that appeared on most of our anniversary cards for the last decade:

Two are better than one. . . .
For if they fall, one will lift up his companion.
But woe to him who is alone when he falls,
For he has no one to help him up. (Ecclesiastes 4:9–10)

Amen to that, girlfriend. Especially when you fall in a heap.

Chapter 11

🐝

Humor and Children: Cute, Very Cute

*Families with babies and families without babies
are sorry for each other.*
—Ed Howe

I have three children under four years of age," writes Cathy. "I love them, but I *need* to laugh because sometimes I feel like screaming."

Yes, we understand completely.

Ellen from Pennsylvania remembers stopping at a family-run café while on vacation. The manager's six-year-old son, apparently accustomed to having the run of the place, plunked himself down at their table and immediately began a one-way conversation, describing the most intimate and embarrassing details of his family life.

After this went on for several minutes, the boy began yet another topic. "My daddy has a pain—"

Goaded beyond endurance, Ellen's husband retorted, "And I know just who it is!"

Good News/Bad News

Lori from Texas was just learning to walk when her mother put her in a pair of shoes and stood her up. Lori took one step and fell down. Her mother picked her up, and again, little Lori took one step and tumbled down. This went on all day.

The new mother panicked and dragged her off to the emergency room, certain her daughter was paralyzed. The doctor took off the toddler's shoes and she promptly took off across the room. One peek in the shoes revealed the problem—a rock.

Lynne from Pennsylvania had a quiet little kindergartner. Her daughter's teacher insisted the shy student would raise her hand in class, "When she's good and ready."

One day, she was ready.

Officer Friendly came to class to teach the children about saying no to drugs and alcohol. As the teacher explained after school, the young girl had finally raised her hand to tell Officer Friendly, "My mom drinks and drives."

Lynne gasped, "She did what? I don't drink and drive."

Her daughter insisted, "Yes, you do, Mom. Every day you drink your coffee when you drive me to school."

Pearls of Wisdom

Lori from Illinois has a sister-in-law who's a high school counselor and thus knows all the signs of emotional upheaval. One morning her preteen daughter showed up for breakfast, dragging her feet and rubbing her eyes. The young girl flopped down in her chair and told her mother she was sick of life.

All of her mother's high school counselor alarms went off as she rushed around the breakfast bar, put an arm around her daughter, and began to explain to her why life is worth living.

The daughter looked up at her with a confused look on her face. "Mom!?! I meant Life cereal."

Who ever thought cereal could be such a cause for concern? Young David was only two when he looked down at the milk in his cereal bowl and exclaimed, "The cereal ate my milk." His mother Kathy admits, "I think he was a little anxious about cereal after that. It looks harmless, but don't turn your back on it!"

Thanks, I Didn't Need That

Our offspring know just the right thing to say or do to make us smile—most of the time. Glenda's sixteen-year-old daughter watched her mom moping around with a glum face the week before reaching the big 5-0.

"What's wrong, Mom?" the teenager asked.

"I'm depressed about my birthday because it means half my life is over."

"Oh, no, Mom," she assured her. "It's probably more than half your life because most people don't live to be a hundred." Then seeing the look of horror on her mother's face, she started backpedaling. "Unless, of course, you live to be as old as Grandma Carrie, who was 101 when she died. So, let's see, that gives you another six months until half your life is over."

As Glenda says, "There's no comfort like having a teenager in your old age."

Cindy from Georgia values humor in her house. Since she's "a special education teacher and the mother of two teenage boys," laughter helps her cope. Or as Deana put it, "I'm a social worker and a single parent of a fourteen-year-old daughter— need I say more?"

No, that does it.

Marilyn from Michigan hasn't had much support from her teenagers, either. She recalls a time when her thirteen-year-old daughter was taking critical inventory of her mother's fashion sense.

"Mom, that outfit you're wearing looks like it's from the sixties. And your hair needs some work. It looks greasy. And your complexion is awful!"

My, how affirming. Then her eleven-year-old son leaned forward and said very seriously, "Yeah, you ought to use some Oil of Old Lady."

Guarding Our Reputations

Rick from California worked side by side with Gary in police work, and their families became very close. "But as the years passed, our careers went in different directions—Gary's to vice and narcotics enforcement, mine to robbery/homicide investigations. It wasn't long before Gary had the long hair and beard of an officer in deep cover, and our families didn't get to see each other as often as we wanted to."

One day their five-year-old daughters were playing together. Rick's daughter, Erin, passed by a picture of her friend's father as a rookie police officer in uniform—all spit, polish, and short hair. "Kerry, who is that?"

"That's my daddy, back when he used to wash his face and comb his hair."

Sanctified Silliness

Since we usually think of church as a serious place, it's doubly funny when humor happens there.

We all know what the Good News is, but in Susan's South Dakota household, it has additional significance.

Her preschooler had an extreme case of constipation. The doctor suggested all the usual remedies, including mineral oil, enemas, and finally a saline solution, which did the trick.

"Mom, I have good news," her son called out. *Good news* became his phrase to signal a successful bowel movement.

During the children's sermon one Sunday, the minister asked, "Does anyone know what *Good News* means?" Susan's son quickly raised his hand.

The really good news is, the minister called on someone else.

At Molly's church, it was traditional when someone had a birthday to sing "Happy Birthday to You" as that person went forward and put a penny for each year of age in the offering plate.

Their four-year-old son, Bren, had his four pennies, but he also had a problem. Molly writes, "When it was time for the great event, I turned to him and smiled, motioning toward the front of the church. Then I looked down and saw that Bren had hooked the toy handcuffs he got for his birthday to one hand and one leg."

No birthday offering, no song, no going forward for Bren, while his parents laughed hysterically and tried to locate the key.

After the service was over, they finally found it. In his pocket.

Yet a third minor challenge at church turned Suzann's day into a blush fest. Her seven-year-old daughter, Megan, had gone to Sunday school that morning, where her teacher presented a lesson on servanthood.

"Have any of you been helpful recently?" the teacher wanted to know.

Megan nodded and raised her hand. "My mother lost her bra this morning, and I helped her look for it. I finally found it in the dirty clothes, but she said it wasn't really that dirty, so she put it on and wore it to church today."

Oh, now that was helpful.

Just as Bill and I don't put all our "joy expectations" on each other, we don't insist that our kids bring us a reason to laugh every minute either. We're simply grateful when they do make us laugh, which is delightfully often.

Kinda balances things out, don't you think?

THE FAMILY CIRCUS®   **By Bil Keane**

"Anytime you're ready, Daddy, I'll be
sitting outside growing older."

Growing Up with Humor

The healthiest families have lots of inside jokes, humor that's communicated with a single word, an expression, a gesture. I remember a basket that my mother often used for serving dinner rolls and such. The person who designed it obviously never tried to pick it up by the handle, which was shaped like the letter *C*.

The first time my brother Tom grabbed the basket to pass the rolls at Thanksgiving—woops!—down swung the basket and down went the rolls, right in the gravy bowl. It became a 'trick" basket we loved to use when company came. I've inherited it, along with all the happy memories.

Children are born with a sense of humor already built into their hard drives. But more serious-natured parents and siblings can sometimes belittle that playfulness until it quietly gets deleted like an old computer file. What weary parent hasn't at one time or another squashed the spirit of a noisy, giggling child by intoning, "Wipe that smile off your face . . ." or "You think you're sooo funny" . . . or "It's not polite to laugh here."

The kids get the message: Don't be funny around Mom and Dad. They don't get it!

Our disciplinary ways can be pretty amusing, though, and not necessarily by intent. Sandy's mother was always mixing metaphors and would often toss them into her lectures. Sandy remembers, "One day she was giving us three girls a stern talking to about patience, and she said, 'Don't count your chickens until they get across the bridge.' Naturally, we all dissolved into laughter while our poor mother was mystified and more than a little miffed that we weren't taking her lecture more seriously."

Now as adults, the don't-count-your-chickens thing has become one of their family watchwords. Sandy explains, "If one of us is trying to rush God's timing for our lives, another of us will say, 'Don't count your chickens until they get across the bridge,' and it immediately tells us to chill out and wait for God. In his time, those old chickens will get across that bridge and so will we, with no need to worry about the troubled waters underneath! Besides, it always makes us laugh, and that usually fixes whatever's bothering us. Mom is gone now, but her joy and laughter live on. Humor is one of the few things in life that endures."

Sibling Rivalry in the Making

Bonnie had seven brothers, none of whom came to her rescue when she got in deep water on the family farm. As she tells the tale, "One day as my father was leaving for work, he told me to water the rabbits. I hated the barn and everything in it, including the rabbits, so I paid one of my brothers a dollar to water the rabbits for me."

When her dad returned home from work, he asked, "Did you water the rabbits?"

"Yes," Barbara fibbed.

"What did you use to water them?" he wanted to know.

"I used the same bucket we always use."

"Oh, really? And how did you manage to get the bucket out of the trunk of my car while I was at work?"

The Bible says, "Your sin will find you out." In this case, the rabbits survived and so did Bonnie's sense of humor. She also assures us, "I don't think I ever told him another lie!"

Elaine's family didn't mean to get her in hot water, either, but did they ever. She was the director of religious education at her church, and since it was late November, she was going to show "A Charlie Brown Thanksgiving," which she'd taped.

She popped the video in for the children, then went to help another teacher. Suddenly the teen helpers came running to get her, shouting about naked people on the video.

Snoopy without clothes, maybe, but Charlie Brown?

Elaine ran back into the room to find an R-rated movie on the screen with a man and a woman naked in a Volkswagen. Her face turned red, and she jerked the offensive video out and promptly put in a cartoon video of the creation story. "That way," she reasoned, "if the children remembered a naked couple, I hoped it would be Adam and Eve. I learned two valuable lessons: (1) Stay in the room until the show starts, and (2) never let your family record a movie on a tape you plan to use for church!"

We'll certainly make a note of that.

Squeaky Clean

One evening after a particularly trying day at work, Jeanne was preparing dinner to the sounds of her two sons picking at each other and calling each other nasty names. She kept telling them to quit arguing and reminding them, "We don't call each other names." Did this stop them? "Get real," Jeanne advises.

Finally she'd had enough. "I flew back to their room and told them in a very loud tone of voice that if I heard one more person call anyone a name other than their given Christian name, I was going to wash his mouth out with soap! I warned them that my mother had done this once to me and it was not pleasant."

As she tromped back through the dining area toward the kitchen, she thought she heard her husband make some sort of comment from the TV room. She whirled back into the doorway, fixed him with a glare, and demanded, "Would you repeat that comment?"

"Honey, I didn't say anything."

"Yes, you did," she insisted. "What was it?"

But she didn't really need to hear it again. She had heard him say the first time that he didn't want soap in his mouth.

This only threw fuel on her fire, and she started berating this poor hapless man for making fun of her when she was trying to correct the boys.

Her husband suddenly started rolling with laughter, tears streaming from his eyes.

"Now what's so funny?" she demanded to know.

"I didn't say 'I didn't want soap in my mouth.' What I said was, 'I didn't once open my mouth.'"

Jeanne laughed until she cried. "It was just what I needed to get rid of the stress of the day. This little story has been told throughout my family, and whenever someone really needs a laugh all we have to say is, 'I didn't want soap in my mouth!'"

All in the Family

Siblings do lose their sense of humor on occasion. One such occasion comes to mind immediately. It was Friday evening and we were on a family outing. Why are these supposed to be fun? Four people, various suitcases, jammed together in a car at the end of a wearying week.

To add to the angst, I was not in good spirits. Was, in fact, cranky, which turns up the volume on Bill's whine-o-meter too. But hey, the kids started it. They were in the backseat, behaving like kids:

"Eeeek, she touched me!"

"Did not!"

"Did too. Move your leg!"

"That's your leg on my side of the car."

Life as usual, in other words. Bill and I were not doing much better in the front seat. I love this man with all my heart, but he was getting on the one nerve I had left. Things heated up to such a pitch that I finally zipped my lips and swung my head around to look out the window of the car.

I was not looking for anything in particular, I just didn't want to look at him. The next words he says better be *I'm sorry,* I fumed to myself.

We passed a Wal-Mart, and the letter *l* had fallen off the sign. That's where we oughta shop tonight, I thought. *Wa*-Mart. Because that's exactly what this car sounds like. Wa-wa-wa!

Suddenly, the kids got quiet in the backseat, and an ominous silence filled the car. You know how it is when you've had words with someone. The tension fills the atmosphere around you with a heaviness that you can almost touch.

Wise Bill decided to cut the tension with the knife of humor. He turned to my back and gave me a full-throttle raspberry. *Thhhwwwppp!*

Bill later told me it was the riskiest thing he'd ever done. Introducing humor at a stressful family moment is dangerous, but the rewards can be well worth the risk.

Since I literally did not see it coming, I cracked up. Exploded with laughter. Relieved, so did Bill. You could feel the tension between us leak out the bottom of the car. We were in love again. We were even in like again.

Meanwhile, in the backseat, the kids kept right on whining. But the two passengers up front had learned a valuable lesson: Life with children goes better with laughter. Betty from Pennsylvania says, "Humor is a bond in my family. My children all say we didn't have much money when they were growing up, but my husband passed on our sense of humor to them."

Dollars and cents pale in value next to a sense of humor.

If you're a laughing parent, your children will be laughing siblings, who marry laughing spouses, who give birth to laughing grandchildren. It's worth the investment.

CHAPTER 12

🐝

Humor and Friendship: Friends Laugh with Their Elbows

You can always tell a real friend: When you've made a fool of yourself he doesn't feel you've done a permanent job.
—Laurence J. Peter

"I tend to surround myself with friends who have been generously blessed with the art of humor," says Leslie from North Carolina. "They keep me in stitches most of the time, but also help me to stay grounded and feeling great."

And friends do laugh with their elbows. I've watched 'em out there in the audience, elbowing, rubbing shoulders, leaning into one another, playing footsie, even just winking across the table. "Are you getting this?" their eyes say silently to one another. When something funny happens, we always turn first to a friend to share it.

Friendships occur at different levels, from acquaintances to colleagues to best buddies. They differ in number, from the packs we traveled in through school, to the deeper, one-on-one friendships that lasted long past graduation.

A schoolteacher in Florida knows the value of laughter to both build friendships and overcome peer pressure at its most painfully embarrassing. Twyla teaches high school, "where every student must be cool at all times."

Yes, we remember those days.

As she describes it, "The bell was ringing, and one of my students ran blindly down the hall to make it to class on time. As she crossed the threshold, she stumbled on the carpet edge. Books, arms, and legs flew in every direction. Here was this poor child, prostrate in front of her peers."

We feel her pain. Ouch.

"The room was deadly silent, and suddenly my laughter broke the tension. As we laughed and then cried, we finally remembered to see if the girl was okay—she was! The important lesson for that day was not learning U.S. History, but learning to stop taking ourselves so seriously."

I remember all my friends through the years, those one-at-a-time special friends. Through school, it was Elaine, Donna, Judy, and Sue. Through my single years, it was Melinda and Debra. More recently, it was Kathy and Pam, when we each shared a pregnancy together. Now *that's* a humor-based experience.

When women marry, their friendships go through a transitional stage. The new bride drops out of circulation for a season, until the honeymoon is over—both literally and figuratively! No matter how great a man she married, eventually she may discover that her husband just isn't "wired" to meet all her emotional needs.

Example: Let's say I'm chewing over something that happened, some little unpleasant thing that keeps turning over and over in my mind. I tell my dear Bill about it, blow by blow: "Then she said . . .then I said . . ."

He listens for about four minutes, gives me a simple solution, and changes the subject.

Wait! I didn't need a solution. I've already thought of six of those myself. I just needed to talk it over with someone.

Exactly. What I needed was a friend. A woman who understands precisely the scenario I'm describing and gives me the only thing I really needed—her ears and her nodding head.

And her laughing lips.

Shared Funny Experiences

I'm convinced the primary glue in a woman-to-woman friendship is a compatible sense of humor, the ability to steer each other through the deep waters of life in a tugboat called *Shared Funny Experiences*. Usually you each take turns at the helm: You cry, I'll laugh, then I'll remind you when you laughed, and pretty soon, we'll both be in stiches again.

Aren't you intuitively drawn to someone who looks at life with your same warped sense of humor? My friend Frani, who has a smile that can light a room like a 100-watt bulb, says, "I love seeing a person laugh. It changes their entire appearance, makes them accessible. You look forward to being with people who can see the humorous sides of life because they make life fun."

Lisa from Kentucky thinks the only thing more enjoyable than remembering something funny that happened "is reminiscing with a witness, someone who was there when it happened. The story always gets more embellished that way and seems more hysterical."

Andrea from Pennsylvania remembers the year a group of friends went to a small camp for a weekend retreat. "We arrived after dark, so we couldn't see any of the grounds other than where we shone our flashlights.

"Five of us set out to find the girls' rest room. The building was very dark, but as we got closer, a motion light came on. Mere feet away stood a doghouse with a huge black dog lurking in the shadows. We all started screaming and ran past the dog into the bathroom. Our screams turned to laughter when, by the light of day, we realized that the ferocious dog was only a wooden silhouette!"

It's Four O'Clock—Do You Know Where Your Friend Is?

Ronda from New Mexico had friends standing by when she arranged a date with a man she met through a classified ad in the newspaper.

She explains, "My list of the perfect mate was narrowed down to five points: (1) a Christian, (2) cares about other people, (3) loves his parents, (4) likes to travel, and (5) has a sense of humor."

In his first message to her, he explained that he (1) was active in his church, (2) was a volunteer fireman and EMT, (3) had parents in Pennsylvania, (4) was retired Navy and owned a motor home, and (5) definitely had a sense of humor.

They met for lunch at 1:00, while her friends fretted about her safety. When Ronda and her date didn't leave the restaurant until 4:30, she had to "race home to call my two friends who were alerted to where and what I was doing. They were to call the police if I wasn't home by 4:00, fearing that I'd been abducted, raped and murdered," in that order!

Susan from Oregon watched a friend turn green one Easter, right before her eyes. Susan and Karen were dying Easter eggs with the kids and warned them to "be careful or you'll get dye everywhere."

Susan was on one side of the table, with Karen directly across from her. Susan decided there wasn't enough green dye in the water, so she squirted some food coloring in the direction of the bowl.

Oops.

She squeezed too hard, the end of the bottle came off, and Karen became green. And as everyone knows, it's not easy being green.

Susan confessed, "She had to go to church the next morning, still green. We laugh about it to this day. I think that's the only time I've seen her turn green over anything!"

Same holiday, whole different story.

Judy from Texas, along with her husband, flew to Washington, D.C., to visit their daughter, Laurel, for Easter. Judy and hubby rented a car and had Laurel drive them everywhere sightseeing, including Mount Vernon, Georgetown, and Old Alexandria, where Judy bought her daughter a beautiful Easter basket filled with bath products.

After a nice dinner, they headed back to Laurel's townhouse. As they approached the door, Judy saw a strange look appear on her daughter's face.

"What's wrong?" Judy asked.

Laurel gulped. "My keys are in my house, and my roommate is in New Jersey."

"Do your neighbors have a key?"

"Yes, but they are in West Virginia for Easter."

"Call a locksmith," said her father, sounding fatherly.

But no one would come until Monday morning. Meanwhile, it was 11:00 on a Saturday night, Easter eve, and the snow was deepening.

Then Laurel remembered that there was a Realtor lockbox on their door because the house was for sale. Laurel called the Realtor and arranged to get the key. Now the other shoe dropped.

"For safety reasons the lockbox has a timer on it," the Realtor explained, "and it will not open between 10:00 P.M. and 8:00 A.M. See you in the morning."

Cold, tired, and frustrated were just a few of the things they were feeling. The threesome drove to a nearby Holiday Inn and threw themselves on the mercy of the desk clerk, who gave them a room at a discount because of their dilemma.

By the time they got to the room, hubby was fuming, daughter was on the verge of tears, and Mom began to laugh. They looked at her in astonishment

"What is so funny?" they demanded.

"We are," she said. "Look at us. We're on an adventure that was not of our choosing, so let's make the best of it. Thou shalt not whine."

She emptied her purse on the bed and began to dig. "My God shall supply all our needs," she insisted, pulling out three minted toothpicks (unused), three Certs to save for morning, two aspirin (she gave them to her husband at once), a sample night cream, and three chocolate mints, which she placed on the pillows.

Plus, there were all those lovely bath things in the Easter basket. They bathed (one at a time, of course) in fragrant style.

Judy shares, "The last sound I heard as I drifted to sleep was my husband's chuckle. We awoke to a beautiful Easter morning, met the Realtor, and got in the house in time to dress and get to church. As we entered the sanctuary my daughter said, 'Look at these people. I wonder if any of them had as much trouble as we did just getting here?!'"

This trio will never be the same after such an experience. We'd never choose these challenges, but when they happen and we make the most of it, like Judy did, it creates memories that build strong families and strong friendships. As Jan from Nevada sees it, "Laughter creates a powerful energy that connects people and situations."

Blown Away

Speaking of powerful energy, Karla from Texas went to see the movie *Twister* with two friends. She was nervous about the whole thing, since she'd been through three real tornadoes.

Yikes.

Karla worked up her courage, walked into the theater with her friends, and was soon engrossed with the edge-of-seat action on screen. The biggest challenge was the soundtrack, which was a little too realistic in volume and intensity for Karla.

During an especially dramatic scene, a sudden flash of lightning shot Karla out of her seat, jumping, hollering, and unintentionally kicking the seat in front of her. Startled, the man sitting there yelled and launched his popcorn across the aisle, hitting another woman, who in turn jumped up and tossed her soda in the air.

This started a chain reaction along the entire right side of the theater, sending people and popcorn flying with abandon.

The producers of *Twister* didn't know they had a comedy on their hands, but that day in that Texas movie theater, the laugh was on them.

When we rent the video to watch at home, I'm inviting Karla.

Cathy from Oklahoma is welcome to join us, since she agrees, "I love humor, and I love people with a good sense of humor. I think life would be pretty dull without it."

What Is Your Favorite Funny Book?

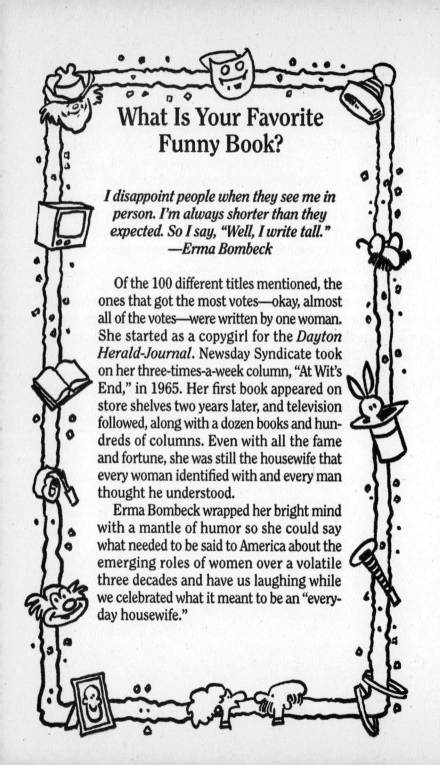

I disappoint people when they see me in person. I'm always shorter than they expected. So I say, "Well, I write tall."
—*Erma Bombeck*

Of the 100 different titles mentioned, the ones that got the most votes—okay, almost all of the votes—were written by one woman. She started as a copygirl for the *Dayton Herald-Journal*. Newsday Syndicate took on her three-times-a-week column, "At Wit's End," in 1965. Her first book appeared on store shelves two years later, and television followed, along with a dozen books and hundreds of columns. Even with all the fame and fortune, she was still the housewife that every woman identified with and every man thought he understood.

Erma Bombeck wrapped her bright mind with a mantle of humor so she could say what needed to be said to America about the emerging roles of women over a volatile three decades and have us laughing while we celebrated what it meant to be an "everyday housewife."

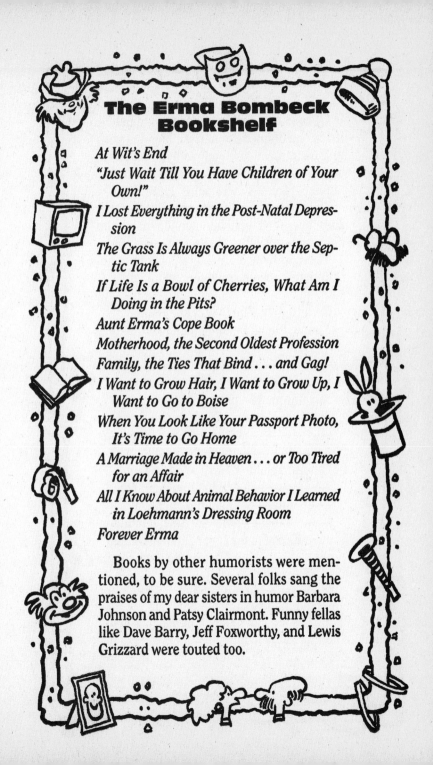

The Erma Bombeck Bookshelf

At Wit's End

"Just Wait Till You Have Children of Your Own!"

I Lost Everything in the Post-Natal Depression

The Grass Is Always Greener over the Septic Tank

If Life Is a Bowl of Cherries, What Am I Doing in the Pits?

Aunt Erma's Cope Book

Motherhood, the Second Oldest Profession

Family, the Ties That Bind . . . and Gag!

I Want to Grow Hair, I Want to Grow Up, I Want to Go to Boise

When You Look Like Your Passport Photo, It's Time to Go Home

A Marriage Made in Heaven . . . or Too Tired for an Affair

All I Know About Animal Behavior I Learned in Loehmann's Dressing Room

Forever Erma

Books by other humorists were mentioned, to be sure. Several folks sang the praises of my dear sisters in humor Barbara Johnson and Patsy Clairmont. Funny fellas like Dave Barry, Jeff Foxworthy, and Lewis Grizzard were touted too.

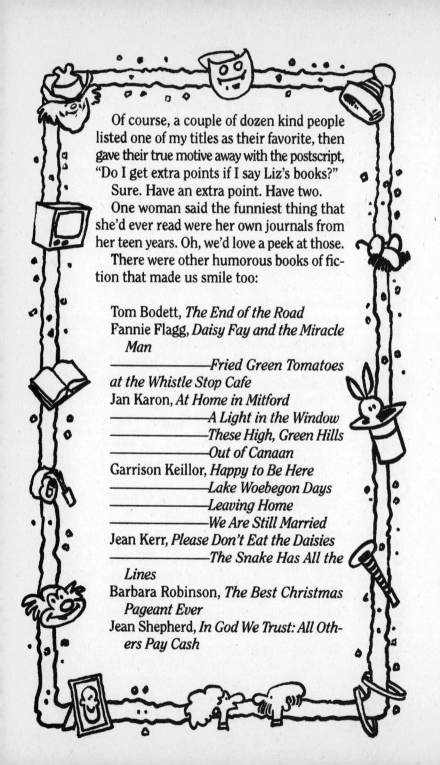

Of course, a couple of dozen kind people listed one of my titles as their favorite, then gave their true motive away with the postscript, "Do I get extra points if I say Liz's books?"

Sure. Have an extra point. Have two.

One woman said the funniest thing that she'd ever read were her own journals from her teen years. Oh, we'd love a peek at those.

There were other humorous books of fiction that made us smile too:

Tom Bodett, *The End of the Road*
Fannie Flagg, *Daisy Fay and the Miracle Man*
——————*Fried Green Tomatoes at the Whistle Stop Cafe*
Jan Karon, *At Home in Mitford*
——————*A Light in the Window*
——————*These High, Green Hills*
——————*Out of Canaan*
Garrison Keillor, *Happy to Be Here*
——————*Lake Woebegon Days*
——————*Leaving Home*
——————*We Are Still Married*
Jean Kerr, *Please Don't Eat the Daisies*
——————*The Snake Has All the Lines*
Barbara Robinson, *The Best Christmas Pageant Ever*
Jean Shepherd, *In God We Trust: All Others Pay Cash*

CHAPTER 13

ॐ

Humor and Work: Funny Business Is Good Business

Did you hear about the cannibal who was fired from his job?
He got caught buttering up the boss.
—Gail from Texas

What's so fun about going to work? Everything, if you take your sense of humor with you. "Give me laugh lines any old day rather than two exclamation marks in the center of my forehead from frowning over a computer screen," laughs Frani from California. "I love to laugh," agrees Brenda from Florida, who works in a health-care setting. "We laugh a lot at work. A good sense of humor helps everybody—patients and staff."

Good thing that Brenda didn't work for the same employer that Brenda from Indiana did: "My sour supervisor told me I laughed too much. I was pleased with that 'fault'!"

She laughed too much? How much is too much? Too much to get her work done? Maybe not. Since laughter relieves stress and promotes communication, it brings more productivity to the workplace, not less. Too much to keep customers happy? Are you kidding? As long as employees know what they're doing, people who make doing business fun will always attract customers.

The key is that the humor be inclusive of the customer, as opposed to employees standing around cutting up with coworkers rather than taking care of business. If you can make it fun for you and for the other person across the counter, across the desk, or on the other end of the phone, then customers will beat a path to your door.

Although my clients hire me to help them laugh, sometimes they toss a giggle in my direction. Pat in Michigan wrote to inform me that I would be met at the airport by a limousine service. "They also operate a funeral home," she warned me, "so make sure you are upright at all times. We don't want them to get their wires crossed!"

What, and die laughing?

Leading by Example, Sort of

No wonder my brother had an I-Like-Ike button in the fifties. Dwight D. Eisenhower is the one who said, "A sense of humor is part of the art of leadership, of getting along with people, of getting things done."

Jody from Iowa led with laughter in her stint as a supervisor over several floors of a major department store in Cedar Rapids. "It was not uncommon for me to put in ridiculous hours and at odd times. One night I stayed late and decided to rearrange everything. Once I get an idea, I'm off and running and can't stop. I was moving clothing racks, switching wall displays, taking pipes off walls, you name it. Clothes were everywhere. It was a mess!"

Her buddies in the janitorial service knew she was doing her usual goofing around and so didn't keep track of her while they were busy cleaning. She disappeared into one of the many back rooms to put away some of the mess and didn't notice the door close behind her. She found the new fixtures she was looking for, went back to the door and, "You guessed it. The door was locked."

She did what anyone would do at 3:00 in the morning, locked in the back room of a department store: "I pounded and pounded and pounded and, well, you get the picture."

Yes, we do.

"I heard vacuuming in a nearby department, so I found the phone and called. It rang and rang and rang and, well, you get my drift."

Yes, we do.

"Now panic set in. I have been at the store for eighteen hours, so you can imagine what I looked like, especially after dragging around clothing and fixtures for the last six hours. Not a pretty sight.

"What were my options? I could call and wake up my sister and brother-in-law, so one of them could come down and try to get the janitors' attention from the front entrance." Maybe not. "There was a window in the back room, and I could get it open, but it's a long way down. What if I fell and hurt myself? What if someone saw me and called the police?"

Her imagination was running full tilt by this time. "Why aren't they worried about me out there? What about the mess I still have to clean up? What will they say when they see me looking the way I do? Is there any way I could just slip out in the morning?"

She tried the phone again, pounded on the door again, and worried some more. "What will my superiors say when they find out? What if the newspaper gets wind of this story, because 911 may be the only way out."

Jody finally decided to get on her knees and pray. "Within minutes, the one woman who was in charge came yelling my name. I jumped up and yelled 'I'm in here!' I did not know whether to die of embarrassment or rejoice. I decided to rejoice."

She has a kindred spirit in Laurie from North Carolina who says, "I've been a manager for almost thirty years. It is a very stressful job. Humor has been my stress relief—after prayer, of course."

Humor and the
Trickle-Down Theory

It wouldn't hurt to pray for a sense of humor for your own boss. Loretta is grateful her supervisor had one in her time of need. The year was 1961. As Loretta says, "All the characters are now deceased except me. Therefore, I can tell the story for the first time.

"I'd just graduated from college and was executive secretary to the plant manager of the Tappan Company. The plant manager asked that I write a letter to President Tappan and Vice President Webster asking them and their wives to attend a weekend celebration for the top salespeople. First I typed the letter to Mr. Webster (keep in mind that there were no word processors in 1961), asking that he and Mrs. Webster attend the special event. Then I typed the letter to Mr. Tappan, inadvertently forgetting to change the wife's name.

"We soon had a response to the invitation from Mr. Tappan. I was called to the big corner office, and my plant manager let me read Mr. Tappan's letter: 'We will happily attend the weekend gathering. Even though my wife and I are very fond of Mrs. Webster, my wife is narrow-minded and will not let me spend the weekend with Mrs. Webster!'"

Here's to any CEO who can tee-hee-ho.

Lawyers have a reputation for being humor impaired, but Pamela from Tennessee is happy to toss that stereotype out the window. "I was representing the plaintiff, and the defendant insisted he didn't need an attorney and would represent himself."

His first mistake.

"Every time I asked him a question, he asked me a question. I explained very nicely that he was required to answer my questions but that I did not have to answer his questions. The defendant became so agitated that the judge had to give him the same instructions about answering my questions."

His second mistake.

Finally, she asked the defendant, "What is your reputation for truthfulness in the community?"

At this point the man was so unnerved that he turned to the judge and asked, "What does the truth have to do with this?"

Case closed.

Don't Go Away Mad, Just Go Away

Pam and her husband were newlyweds when they went to one of those home-and-garden shows, with vendors from landscaping to mortgages, insurance to water systems. "We signed up for all the free stuff we could get. One guy we talked to for a really long time—not our choice, we couldn't get away—was named Mike Moss, who sold insurance. We finally gave him our phone number just to get away from him."

Uh-oh.

"Sure enough, a day later we got a call from Mike Moss. My husband was out in the yard, so I decided to do the 'grown-up thing' and ask him not to call again. I told him in no uncertain terms we were not interested in hearing from him or having anything to do with his company."

"Does your husband know you are saying this?" he had the nerve to ask.

"Of course he does; it was his idea!" she declared, her feathers ruffled, and hung up.

"I went out and told my husband what had happened and waited to hear how proud he was of me. All I got was a really strange look."

"Who called?" hubby wanted to know.

"Mike Moss."

Her husband suddenly ran inside to use the phone. Seems that one of his foremen—a Mike Moss—had said he might call that weekend for overtime work. "And I'd told my husband's boss we weren't at all interested in his company!" Pam frets. "Finally, my husband was able to straighten it all out, but his boss—the *real* Mike Moss—never did see the humor in it."

Techno Babble

I've always been the last woman I know to "go techno" about anything. I resisted personal computers until I married Bill— Dr. Geek—who assured me that when I turned the PC off at night, all the words would not leak out. Then when everyone started wearing beepers, I was left out in the cold—hey, I'm self-employed, who would beep me? At corporate speaking engagements, where audience members were constantly getting beeped, I felt so intimidated that I considered wearing my garage door opener.

Next I dragged my feet about going online, until I realized that it's a way to talk long-distance for (almost) free. Sign me up.

Then I fought the cellular phone phenomenon, finally succumbing when a slick salesman rattled off dozens of benefits. The only advantage I can find is one he didn't even mention: If someone calls me, I can find my purse.

Girlfriend, I'm so low-tech, I didn't even have a color television until I married one in 1986.

So when the facsimile machine showed up in my Christmas stocking a few years ago, I wasn't convinced that I had any use for it. Hadn't we been doing business for centuries without one?

It was unimpressive looking at best. A big phone with too many buttons and an appetite for expensive rolls of oddly scented paper. "Just wait," my friends assured me. "When you put a piece of paper in it, it comes out in California."

"No, it does not," I argued, pointing down. "It comes out all over the floor, which is not in Pasadena."

Like I said, I'm slow on the techno.

From the moment I received my first incoming fax, though, and realized what a handy device this would be, I was sold.

My home office would never be the same. With a beep and a flourish, memos, letters, and—how lovely—product orders slithered out of our phone-on-a-box at all hours of the day and night. No charge, no fuss, no trip to the post office.

The first few days after our machine arrived, I would dash to its side at the first telltale tone, anxious to see who was "talking" to me, fax to fax. Like the calculator, the PC, and the VCR before it, the facsimile machine had me walking around shaking my head, saying, "How did we survive without it?"

I'll tell you how we survived. Beautifully. In the pre-faxable era, procrastinators like me could always buy a little time with, "I'll put that in the mail first thing tomorrow" or "Gosh, I don't know where that paperwork could be. Have you checked your mailroom?"

Such stalling devices are history, my dear. In the archives. A fond memory. Never mind Two-Day Air or Priority Overnight, everybody wants it right now, if not yesterday.

Pressure City.

And, remember those *C*s we earned in penmanship? We figured we'd quickly graduate to a typewriter, then a PC, and never look back. Mr. Fax has fixed us good. Those *C*s look like honor-roll material compared to some of the handwritten coversheets that have glided silently out of my machine. More than once I've had to call the sender (long distance, of course) to ask for their secret deciphering code. Sometimes you wonder if a simple phone call, human to human, might have been more efficient in the first place.

What really worries me is the insistence of today's techno-wizards that soon we'll all have fax machines in our homes. A chicken in every pot, a fax in every family room.

A nightmare, I'd say. All that beeping and swishing at odd hours. Junk faxes spilling all over the carpet. Spouses faxing each other the latest entries in their Day Runners. Desperate calls from the school lunchroom, "Mom! I forgot my band uniform. Can you fax it to me?"

Never mind late-night trips to the store for baby food or tp, soon it will be midnight runs for fp—fax paper—at the local convenient mart, where two rolls are just $5.99 with your purchase of a Big Gulp. Before long, they'll have fax paper in decorator colors or country floral prints or with inspirational sayings in the margin. Scarier than HAL, I'd say.

When the day of the ubiquitous fax comes, I'll be ready. I have figured out how to tame the thermal paper beast. If someone whines that they've faxed something to me with no response, I'll smile sweetly and say, "Oh, you did? So sorry. I forgot to check the floor."

CHAPTER 14

Humor and Yourself: Coulda Fooled Me

An onion can make people cry, but there has never been a vegetable invented to make them laugh.
—Will Rogers

Your best source of humor is right at the end of your nose. Especially if you're looking in a mirror. Karla from Texas said it best: "If I can't laugh at myself, who will? I love to laugh!" And Julie from Michigan insists she has to laugh "so I don't lose my mind—or what's left of it."

The ability to laugh at ourselves is a sign of maturity, of healthy self-esteem, of having our priorities straight, which is to say, God on the throne, us on the ground. *Humble, humus, human, humor* . . . words well suited to our earthly imperfections compared to God's heavenly perfection. Our richest resource for laughter can be found in our own merry hearts and lives.

Karen, who is vertically challenged (i.e., petite), says, "My philosophy in life is to laugh at yourself. Don't take yourself so seriously. One of my favorite remarks I make as I'm leaving is, 'See you shortly—but then I do everything that way!'"

A Vegetable Faux Pas

Marsha from New Mexico was a young captain in the Air Force. "In other words, college educated and supposedly somewhat intelligent," she explains with chagrin. "Our office planned to have a picnic. Not being a seasoned cook, I volunteered to bring potato salad, figuring it would be easy to make." She called her mother to get her favorite recipe and was all set.

The day of the picnic came. Someone said, "Hey, Marsha, where did you get this potato salad?"

"It's my mother's recipe. How do you like it?"

"Well, the potatoes are awfully crunchy. Could you have undercooked the potatoes a bit?"

Marsha asked in a puzzled voice, "How could that be? I followed my mother's recipe exactly."

"What was the recipe?" asked another.

Marsha proudly began to recite it: "Dice four to six cold potatoes . . ."

"Did you cook the potatoes?"

"Nooo. The recipe called for cold potatoes, so I put them in the refrigerator to get them cold."

The laughter went on for a long time. Poor Marsha was confused, as there'd never been any mention of cooking them first.

She admits, "The joke was on me. I called my mother to relay the story. She, too, laughed, and asked whether I had ever actually seen her make the potato salad. Apparently not!"

A Floral Faux Pas

Even more emotionally healing than laughing at yourself the moment something happens is continuing to laugh about it as the story is told, year after year. Mae from Texas admits, "My humorous story is embarrassing to me, but my friends enjoy it and love to tell it.

"A few years ago we invited a couple to our home for dinner and they brought me a pot of tulips. They weren't particularly pretty tulips—they were in a clay pot with the bulbs partially sticking up out of the soil and they were an ugly color—

but these were friends whom we saw often, so I wanted to take care of the tulips simply because they were from them.

"I nurtured this plant, watered it faithfully, fed it plant food, set it outside in the spring, and brought it back into the house before the first freeze. I couldn't throw it away as long as it was blooming."

One afternoon about two years later, her youngest son absent-mindedly reached over and rubbed the tulip petals.

"Don't touch those, honey, it could cause spots."

She was stunned by his reply. "Mom, this plant isn't real!"

Sure enough, he was right. For two years Mae had nurtured a silk plant. "It did seem exceptionally hardy," she confesses.

Have a Seat

It was a holiday party the guests would never forget. Brenda from New Jersey arrived at her cousin's apartment, which was packed with partygoers. "The apartment was so small that most of us sat on the floor." How small was it? There was a six-foot hero sandwich standing up in the shower stall!

"Unfortunately, the party was very dull," Brenda reports. "I struck up a conversation with one man in a white leisure suit who looked like an Elvis impersonator. He was a big man and sat on a wooden chair all afternoon. He finally got up from the chair, and I sat down in it. The chair was rickety, but I figured if 'Elvis' sat in it for a few hours, I should be safe.

"I don't remember the joke that was said, but I started laughing, and everyone else laughed even harder when I landed on the floor in the middle of the room! The back of the chair came off, and all four legs went flying across the room in different directions. I landed on the floor, with the only evidence that I was ever sitting on a chair pinned beneath me.

"My cousin called a year later to tell me that he finally found the fourth leg to the chair—behind the couch!"

An Award-Winning Performance

The greatest potential for a humbling, humoring experience may come at the exact moment we are being honored for some outstanding accomplishment. That's the Lord's sense of humor at work, don't you think?

Camille's daughter traveled to Boston to receive a special award from her employer, a pharmaceutical company. Camille tells us, "After my daughter, Liz, received the award, one of the vice presidents of the company stepped over to her table to congratulate her. She reached up to shake hands with him and caught her bracelet on her pantyhose! A friend had to cut a hole in her hose so she could get the bracelet loose. She was so embarrassed—but these things happen to a woman named Liz, right?"

(Gee, I can't imagine having such an embarrassing thing happen to me while wearing pantyhose . . .)

Making a Splashy Entrance

Dennis didn't wait until his employer gave him an award to have his most embarrassing moment—he got it out of the way his very first day on the job.

"Of course, I was unfamiliar with the building, so I had to ask my new supervisor where the rest rooms were located. I found the men's room, put the toilet seat down, and unbuckled my pants, etc. Apparently for hygiene reasons, the toilet seat raised up automatically. So when I sat down, fully expecting the toilet seat to be where I had placed it, instead I plunged end-first into the toilet, splashed water everywhere, and got stuck! It took me thirty long minutes to unwedge myself from the porcelain throne.

"By the time I returned to my desk, I was sweating and my polyester leisure suit was drenched. How embarrassing to have to tell my new supervisor that I got stuck in the toilet!"

We couldn't agree more, Dennis.

The Ball Is in Your Court

"Before I was a true believer, tennis was my god," Karen admits. "It was so important to me that I stuffed skirts under the seat of my car so I wouldn't be caught playing again. Finally I gave up tennis, opting instead for Bible study and walking in the park.

"One day while walking around the track, I saw a group of 'serious' tennis players volleying. The ball came over the top of the fence and onto the track. Wanting to be of assistance, I ran to get the ball, giving them a look of, 'Don't worry, I've got this whole situation under control. Just watch this star athlete in action!'

"I picked up the ball, and while the relieved foursome watched me wind up to throw it, my hand accidently released the ball. It shot backward into the path of a moving truck tire and blew up on impact.

"The five of us stared in disbelief. I finally did what I do best—laugh uncontrollably—while the ladies in snazzy tennis attire shook their heads at the poor fool on the other side of the fence!"

Crime Does Not Play

Rick is a robbery-and-homicide detective in California. He was dispatched to a residential neighborhood where uniformed officers had a robbery suspect in custody. As Rick describes the scene, "The culprit had robbed a popular doughnut shop, then fled on foot as several patrons pursued him. The customers had spaced themselves along the street to direct the police officers, who found the robber hiding in his bedroom."

The crook may not have had much sense of humor about himself, but the doughnut-shop customers thought he was a hoot. "The suspect had skulked into the shop door during the busiest time of the morning. He spun through the door and pulled his disguise over his head—a pillowcase—in which he had neglected to cut out the eye holes!"

Oh, now that is funny.

This living pillowase "stood there and waved a sawed-off shotgun at the clerk as he demanded all the cash. Realizing his error, the crook occasionally lifted the front of the pillowcase from his face, told the patrons to remain seated, and then pulled the pillowcase back over his face."

Gee, what a perfect disguise.

"After securing his ill-gotten booty, the bandit fled on foot, only to be followed home by the plethora of patrons who could easily identify him from the several times he raised his mask!"

Beware of Containers That Burp

Louisiana Patty was a brand-new Tupperware consultant, eager and excited about her second in-home demonstration. "The hostess wanted a baking theme, so I began to demonstrate Tupperware's wonderful piecrust recipe—you simply dump in the ingredients and shake."

In went flour, shortening, and 7UP (!), then she sealed the container and started to shake it. "Everything was going great and I had everyone's attention, when suddenly the top came off and flour and shortening went everywhere—all over the nine guests, all over the hostess's gorgeous emerald carpet, and all over me.

"I was totally stunned and will never forget fluttering my eyelashes with shortening and flour dripping off them."

They always play ice-breaker games at Tupperware parties. Maybe Patty could suggest that one to the home office.

Some Sundays Are Like That

Toni knows all about having one of those pie-crust-in-your-hair kind of days. She explains, "I'm a music director for the 8:00 service at our church. One Sunday I found myself driving to mass in a hurry (I'm perpetually late), rushed into church with my music bag in one hand and guitar in the other, and promptly tripped as I climbed the altar steps, a church full of people watching behind me.

"During the mass, I started to play a song in the wrong key and had to start over, and then, after mass I went to my car only to find it still running with my keys in it! And it was only 9:30 in the morning.

"I hope I will always be able to laugh when I blunder," Toni reflected. "I hope in my busy life I will remember to take time to enjoy life as it speeds by. One day my son, four, asked me, 'Mommy, why do we sing lasagna at church?'

"It took me a minute before I realized what he was referring to. Then I laughed and said, 'We don't sing *lasagna*, we sing *hosanna*. It means "praise God."'"

Make a joyful shout to the LORD, all you lands!
Serve the LORD with gladness.
(Psalm 100:1–2)

PART FOUR

What's Your (Weather) Sign?

We now know seven reasons why we laugh—from being polite to being genuinely amused to everything in between—and we know where we laugh—at home, at play, at work. The time has come to discover how we laugh, along with the varied ways we weather life with our unique humor personalities.

Speaking of weather, there must be a reason why in Eustis, Florida, the local paper displays a weather map with "Yesterday's Temperatures." What exactly would one do with this information?! To whom would one address their complaints? "Sorry, but the thermometer on my porch read two degrees hotter yesterday."

I'm much more of a prognosticator who uses today's information to predict tomorrow's behavior. Meteorologists can do that with the weather, and to the best of my ability, I try to gauge how someone will respond to a particular form of humor based on their distinct personality type.

CHAPTER 15

What's Showing on Your Weather Channel?

Everybody talks about the weather,
but nobody does anything about it.
—Mark Twain

Josh Billings said, "Laughing is the sensation of feeling good all over, and showing it principally in one spot." The spot he's referring to must be our faces, and more specifically, our mouths, but I beg to differ. A dozen years of watching people laugh has convinced me that they laugh in many spots, not just one.

Rainbows and Earthquakers

Some people can be having a great time, yet not a sound leaks from their lips. They may turn a different color—pink, red, and purple are favorite hues among silent laughers. We'll refer to them as *Rainbows*. Other people indulge in vigorous shoulder action or tummy jumping. I call those folks *Earthquakers*, because that's how they laugh, with movement rather than sound. Having been through five earthquakes (albeit at a safe distance from their epicenters), I know the quakes themselves were silent, but the furniture was noisy.

"My biggest laugh is quiet," agrees Tracy. Dollena from Indiana describes her laugh as "deep, long, and past the point of sound." Joanna from Georgia also says her laugh is "silent, with my mouth wide open." Stella from Indiana experiences "complete body shakes," and Stephanie from Michigan admits, "the funnier the story, the more quietly I laugh. People look to see if my shoulders are shaking."

Weather Systems

For the rest of us who are indeed more vocal with our laughter, here are ten ways we'd describe those sounds, in order of popularity among our 500 survey respondents and grouped by the weather system they most resemble.

1. Cumulus Clouds: The Giggle

More than one hundred of us are gigglers. Giggles, like cumulus clouds, pile up and accumulate. The giggle is the most infectious of the bunch. Elaine from Washington says, "My childhood friends would tell me to laugh, and then they would laugh at my laughter."

Sherry from Oregon's "contagious giggle" has been passed around for many a delightful year. And Pat from Michigan's giggles go on and on "until I have tears running down my face." Indeed, if you give cumulus clouds enough time, they'll rain on you as well.

Men and women both giggle, though we often think of it as a girlish sound, simply because it's often high-pitched and cascades like a gentle waterfall. In print, we might capture it as *tee-hee*, though it's more musical than that. Without a doubt, the giggle is one sound that says, "I'm having fun, please join me!"

2. Squall Line: The Howl

Although this is our second most popular style of laughing, only half of us are howlers, compared to the large number of gigglers. The howl is a noisier laugh, sure to draw more attention and elicit all manner of rubbernecking. Howls aren't very short—Karen from Kentucky admits her howl "goes on and on." Another Karen from the Bluegrass State describes her laugh as "a screaming howl, where I lose my breath and wet my pants, all in one motion."

Sorry, we don't have a specific category for that, however weather-related moisture may be.

I'd have to confess that my own laugh is a cross between a howl and a hoot—not to be confused with a hoot owl—and like all howls, it does cause a scene. Sherry from Colorado considers her own howl "totally out of character." In fact, she will perform it "only with family." Even so, onlookers usually exclaim "Oh, no!" or "Oh, dear!"

Loud, sustained, and *unrestrained* are the watchwords here.

3. Wind Shear: The Blast

Of equal frequency with the howl, the blast is usually of shorter duration and—here's the key—is totally unpredictable, showing up out of nowhere, just like the wind shears I've traveled through while hot-air ballooning. (The hot air I've released for the last fortysomething years is another issue altogether.) Iris from Pennsylvania is a blaster, and she says her husband tells her she sounds like Scooby Doo.

Nancy thinks she and her daughter could make a tape of their bouts of blasting. "It would make the whole world laugh with us, as we hit various notes according to how hard we're laughing."

Do they make sheet music for this? "Two Blasts with Oboe," perhaps?

Think *sudden, violent outburst* for this one.

Portia's blast also moves to silence, and she "usually can't breathe." All weather styles contain that possibility, of moving rapidly from one climate to another without warning. It's almost impossible to predict, from a meteorological standpoint, what sound the laugher will return to when the laugher is finally able to breathe again. Stay tuned.

4. Jet Stream: The Whoop

I know what you're thinking: Howls, blasts, whoops—aren't they all the same? Clearly they aren't to our participants, who selected one over the other, for the most part. Then there's Cheri from Florida and her "melodic, whooping blast," which sounds like its own weather system, as does Leigha from Montana's blended laugh that's "between a whoop and a howl."

The very word *whoop* comes from the sound you make when you do it (*onomatopoeia*, for you English majors). It has a sense of eagerness and enthusiasm about it, a war cry for laughter, if you will. Whoop! Let's go! is the sense of it. Pam from Idaho calls her laugh "a burst of happiness," which sounds like *whoopee* to me.

Becky from Ohio thinks her whoop sounds like "a wild turkey"; Wanda from Texas celebrates the "young, vibrant" nature of her own whoop; and Miriam from Indiana says her laugh leaves her in "no man's land"—that silent place again, I suspect, the place between laughing and breathing.

5. Tornado: The Snort

I have a special place in my heart for snorters because, of course, I count myself among them. This isn't a club you join by choice. Rather, the particular way your nose is structured has something to do with it. I think.

Rose from Hawaii is not pleased about her status as a snorter either. "Appalling! Most embarrassing!" she insists. I'll say this about a snort. It isn't contagious, in that others around you will start snorting, but it is so hilariously distinctive that it usually launches those in earshot off on another squall of their own.

A snort stands out in a crowd because of its unusual timbre. While most laughs are in the soprano range, snorts are baritone. Although I prefer to think of them as musical rather than animal, those of us who snort are not the only laughers who draw our inspiration from the barnyard, as these contributors indicate when describing their own laughs:

- A sheep—Shirley from New York
- A woodpecker—Bryan from Alabama
- A horse—Susan from Pennsylvania
- A hen, before and after laying eggs—Deana from Kentucky
- A braying mule—Marbeth from Kentucky

(This last example of four-legged laughter was suggested by Marbeth's husband. Well, the very idea.)

6. Warm Front: The Chortle

Lewis Carroll was fond of this blend of chuckle and snort, which, like the warm front it resembles, is filled with moist air and genuine warmth. One never chortles in disdain. It's a friendly sound, like a chuckle with attitude.

Sue from Ohio describes her own chortle as a "Hee, Hee, Hee" sound, probably with a bit of spacing between them and punctuated by shoulder shakes.

Three dozen of us chortle regularly and seem no worse for wear.

7. Forked Lightning: The Hoot

Here we have the thunderhead of the bunch and, of the ten styles of laughter, the most explosive and sometimes derisive, as in "They hooted their disapproval."

In more recent usage, though, and especially in the South, you'll hear people respond favorably by saying, "What a hoot!" I once had a pastor introduce me to his congregation with, "Please welcome our speaker, Liz Curtis Higgs, a blessed hoot."

Now there's a quote for the next brochure.

8. Sea Breeze: The Melody

There are two dozen singers among us, whose melodic laugh could be captured on a musical staff. Barbara from Washington describes her musical laugh as "like her mother's." Oh, if only we had them both on tape, to compare! But we'll take her word for it.

The lyrical laugh resembles a flute or, even better, a piccolo.

9. Dust Devil: The Gasp

Shorter than all the other laughs described to this point, the gasp has an oh-no! quality. If you're not watching the gasp in progress, you may swing around to be sure the gasper is okay.

Especially if Ann from Kentucky is the one gasping, since she says it's quickly followed by silence. Sheryl from Oklahoma might make you nervous with her gasps, too, since they are, she admits, "multiple."

10. Unstable Air Masses: Seven Varieties

Karen from California shares that she has "a vertical laugh, depending on the intensity of the humor. It can go from a *tee-hee* to a *har-har* in the twinkling of an eye and a simple prat-fall."

When you're under a lot of barometric pressure, often referred to as stress among nonweatherheads, your laughter may be unstable, veering back and forth between some of the following less popular but highly dramatic sorts of laughs:

- The Wheeze (the preferred laugh for fourteen of us)
- The Hiccup (how Clara from Minnesota ends her laughs)
- The Groan (has its own humor line: "Groaners")
- The Cackle (Allison from Idaho favors these)
- The Honk (especially popular with Canadians)
- The Sneer (more visual than audible, and rather unkind)
- The Hiss (for people who laugh through their teeth)

Garlena from Montana had a hard time putting her laugh on paper. "I really don't know what I sound like, but people always recognize me by my laugh."

Laughs are as individual as weather systems, each one created by shifts in temperature—moods, in our case—and affected by the environment around them.

Venus and Mars in the Weather Lab

Do men and women laugh in the same way, at the same things?

I could either write an entire book on the subject, or cut to the chase—no, they do not.

As a woman who speaks primarily to female audiences, I've noticed an interesting phenomenon: If there is even one man in the room, sitting in full view, women will curtail their laughter slightly. If the audience is 25 percent or more men, the effect is even more noticeable. Given half a roomful of men, the women wait hesitantly, watching the men and one another for cues: "Now? Should I risk looking foolish?"

The younger the woman, the more likely she is to stifle her laughter when men are present. On the other hand, a more mature woman often laughs with abandon, which is one of the many benefits of maturity.

Many other humorists have seen this phenomenon as well. Rosita Perez, my *Ishtar* conspirator, finds that "we women spend a lot of our time waiting until whatever feels right to us also feels right to everyone around us." She has discovered that "when a husband is present, the dynamics are very different; women censor themselves."

Judith Tingley, who has a doctorate in psychology, speaks and writes about male-female communications. She has assessed the problem of women who withhold their laughter as "a high need for approval coupled with a low risk-taking propensity." She notes that women are more restrained in most of their nonverbal communication, but especially so in a mixed group.

Clifford Kuhn, a psychiatry professor who does stand-up comedy on the side, sees things a bit differently. He believes that men enjoy humor more when their wives are laughing and that women actually control the audience. "Some comedy writers create material with the woman in mind," he added.

Humorist Hope Mihalap, a veteran of the platform, observes that "men enjoy one-liners, short things, that seem vaguely tough coming from a woman." Women, she's discovered, love a broader style of delivery, with well-developed characterizations, wide gestures, and animated facial expressions.

I say, let's not take any chances. Women need to laugh till they cry and cry till they laugh, slap the table, and throw their hands in the air. Women must give themselves permission to gather together in the name of good health, and laugh the mascara right off their faces, without even one man present to interfere with their fun!

Many of these male-female dynamics aren't present in the home, though. Bill and I laugh with equal abandon around the house, as do most couples. It's the public display of laughter where invisible lines may be drawn.

Of course, I've always been a woman who colored outside the lines, especially when it comes to having fun.

The Four Humor Personalities

So many wonderful books have been written on the subject of personalities or temperaments—Tim LaHaye and Florence Littauer are two of the very best authorities on the four basic types. You may be familiar with their excellent materials or with the D-I-S-C model at your workplace, or the Myers-Briggs Type Indicator, or Hippocrates's theories of the Sanguine, Melancholy, Choleric, and Phlegmatic fluids of the bodies and how they affect our behaviors.

But I'm sure you've never heard of the Four Weather Personalities, my friend, because I made them up! They are easy to remember, highly visual, and *fun*—key word, here. Since people are as variable as the weather, especially when the winds of change blow them off course, I thought these words would lend atmosphere (pun intended) to our consideration of not only how we laugh—what we look and sound like doing it—but what makes us laugh.

Each weather type will have its own chapter, with plenty of humor to illustrate and illuminate. Following are the four weather personalities in a nutshell—Sunny, Cloudy, Stormy, and Foggy.

1. Sunny. Fun-loving, people-oriented, enthusiastic, and energetic, the *Sunny* soul loves life and enjoys being center stage, but hates getting organized, often arrives late, and never remembers names! Sunnies laugh no matter what the weather. Of those surveyed, 32 percent shone like the sun.

2. Cloudy. Serious, purposeful, logical, and neat, the *Cloudy* person is conscientious, thoughtful, and altogether wonder-ful—as long as you don't mind having a moody perfectionist in your midst. Cloudies are saving their laughs for a rainy day. Among our contributors, 28 percent are not convinced every cloud has a silver lining.

3. Stormy. The born leader of the bunch, the *Stormy* sort is a hard-working visionary who gets things done and keeps things moving, someone who isn't too difficult to get along with, as long as you do it their way! Stormies laugh wherever and whenever they feel like it. Some 23 percent of us insisted on being identified with lightning and thunderbolts.

4. Foggy. Everybody's friend, the peace-loving *Foggy* would rather watch than get involved, is a great listener and media-tor, and has a dry sense of humor—when they're not being a wet blanket! As laughers go, Foggies are great smilers. Because they're so quiet, you might not notice the 17 percent among those surveyed who are in a fog.

Which one are you? Only time and reading will tell. Even with the brief introduction above you may be concerned. Can a person be more than one weather personality? Most assuredly. Most of us are a solid mix of two—after all, party sunny/partly cloudy days are common weather patterns. Because of the per-sonality types that surrounded you in your growing years, you may even dabble in a third style, but if you think you are all four, you have a serious personality disorder.

Seek professional help at once.

On second thought, this is a book about humor, so just laugh about it and keep reading. Know this beyond a doubt: All four personalities have strengths and weaknesses, but all are a valuable addition to the human race. We need the Sunnies to be in charge of cheerful, the Cloudies to be in charge of details, the Stormies to be in charge—period—and the Foggies to be in charge of keeping the rest of us from killing one another.

The most important concept here is this: All four weather personalities have a sense of humor. All have the capacity to laugh out loud, and all need as much humor as possible in their lives. What makes us laugh and how we respond to humor is what keeps life interesting—as do cold fronts and dry spells.

CHAPTER 16

❧

The Sunny Sense of Humor: Let a Smile Be Your Umbrella

A good laugh is sunshine in a house.
—William Makepeace Thackeray

Of the four weather personalities, without question the one who has the most fun, day in and day out, is the Sunny, the warmest weather personality.

Sunnies, as the name implies, share many qualities with Mr. Sun himself—they're dazzling, warm, and bright. But yes, you can get a Sunny-burn if you stand too close!

According to the five hundred kind people who responded to the survey, 32 percent of us are Sunnies. Theme song? "Don't Worry, Be Happy!" Slip on your shades and let's take a look at eight traits of the Sunny and their unique spin on humor.

Warm and Outgoing

See that woman at the checkout counter? The one talking to the person in front of her, behind her, the clerk, the bag boy? That's a Sunny in action.

If nobody's listening, she talks to the candy rack.

"Oh, look! I didn't know they had that flavor. Excuse me, Miss, could you hand me one of those, on the bottom? Oh, and look what's in her basket!"

Sunnies make friends instantly. If the Sunny woman at the grocery store has her husband with her, he'll whisper in her ear, "Do we know these people?"

She does now. Sunnies have more signatures in their high school yearbooks than any other weather type, because they know everybody—or at least act like they do.

The Sunny treasures humor because of its social value. What better way to reach out to people than by saying or doing something amusing?

Attention-Getting and Talkative

The minute her teacher asks a question, my daughter Lillian's hand is the first one up. Of course—she's a Sunny. With a bright mind and childlike curiosity, Sunnies love to ask and answer questions, which is why they have no trouble talking to themselves. I always tell people I'm praying under my breath, but half the time I'm carrying on my own conversation. For the Sunny, this isn't psychotic, it's survival. We're always happiest when we're talking.

In fact, the Sunny is the only weather personality that likes voice mail. After all, what does the machine say? "Talk at the beep." We love that. Voice mail beats getting no answer or a busy signal, though I hate the ones that shut off after thirty seconds. I'm just warming up, haven't even said my full name or phone number yet, and then *click*. So embarrassing. I have to call back and say, "Hi, me again . . ." and hope I can get the rest in before I'm beeped into oblivion a second time.

True Confession: I recorded my outgoing voice mail message in a hurry one day and didn't realize until I called back for messages that I'd recorded this message: "At the tone, please leave your beep."

Your what?!

Exactly as requested, there were seven messages in a row, one friend after another, laughing hysterically and shouting, "Beep!"

Miriam from Indiana must be a Sunny.

"I always loved to talk. When I was twelve years old sitting in the backseat of our rather large church, I was talking away when my father, the minister, stopped his message and said, 'Miriam, since you want to talk so much, either come to the pulpit and do my sermon for me, or come to the front and sit with your mother.'"

Miriam admits, "That walk to my mother in the second row was the longest walk I ever took."

Radiant and Friendly

Not only do Sunnies reach out to others, they also draw people to them like a magnet. Their blue-sky view of life and eternal optimism make them a joy to be around—unless you're trying to get a word in edgewise.

Sunnies are generally morning people, eager to start the day, unless they're night owls who talk long after dark. Then their Sunny self hides behind the clouds until midday. Even half-awake they remain friendly, though. Sunnies are people-pleasers and won't risk losing a friend merely from losing sleep.

Sunnies in my audiences like to participate when they get the chance. One time I asked a large group of conference attendees to tell us what unusual things their husbands brought into their honeymoon cottage. One woman raised her hand and said, "Three stuffed moose from Wyoming!"

The audience and I were quite astounded at this unusual decorating challenge. When she came up to me after the event, blushing furiously and looking very guilty indeed, I wondered if she'd not exaggerated just a tad. "You really didn't get three moose from Wyoming, did you?" I said gently.

"No, Liz." She shook her head, eyes downcast. "What I really got were six stuffed ducks from Mexico, but I didn't think anyone would believe me."

Energetic and Spontaneous

The sun is energy itself, and so is the Sunny personality. Ready to try something new at the drop of the hat, and with enough physical and emotional energy to get them through the project, Sunnies embrace change and welcome innovation. They really get excited if those changes include new forms because they can't find the old forms!

If you get the urge to see a movie and it starts in an hour, call a Sunny, especially if it's a comedy. Need instant feedback on an idea? See a Sunny. Want to redecorate your guest room and need a buddy to visit the mall with you? Sunnies are often gifted in color and design. Need someone to proofread your annual report? Oops. Not the Sunny's strong suit.

But shopping? Now there's where we shine. I met a woman named Mary Ann who'd recently moved to Albuquerque. When

I asked her what she thought of the dry southwest, she exclaimed, "Oh, in our neighborhood, we have both a Sam's Club and a Price Club. That's what I call a good climate!"

Colorful and Expressive

You can't have a rainbow without the sun to reflect all the colors in the spectrum. Sunnies are nothing if not colorful, both in style of dress and in vocabulary (not blue language, of course!). Their facial expressions are animated, their body language goes a mile a minute, and sight gags are one of their favorite forms of humor.

Back in high school, Linda from Pennsylvania drove "an old, decrepit Volkswagen Bug. The poor thing was falling apart, mostly because I kept trying to make it fit into spaces that were too small for it, but I loved it. The horn consisted of a big silver disc in the middle of the steering column that looked more like a hub cap than a horn. Many times this apparatus would fall off onto my lap, as other sundry parts did with regularity.

"One day my best friend, Sandy, and I were cruising, and she saw a friend of ours. She said, 'Ooh, there's Ralphie. Blow the horn.'"

Linda couldn't resist the urge. She took off the horn disc and said, "Here, blow it yourself."

"Sandy wasn't aware that the horn came off, and she thought I'd handed her the whole steering wheel! We ended up laughing so hard I nearly wrecked my precious Bug."

Light and Silly

According to Catullus (c. 60 B.C.), "There is nothing more silly than a silly laugh."

I've always loved the word *silly*, until I found out that among other things it means "stunned, dazed, and lacking common sense."

Gee whiz.

The silly Sunny only appears dazed and confused, when in truth they're just easily amused. We love slapstick, visual humor, broad comedy, and pratfalls. It's not that we don't have taste, we just can't help falling down laughing when others . . . fall down.

Deloris from Kansas worked at a home for the elderly with a Sunny friend. "We'd always think of silly things to do to cheer up the residents," she explained. "I bought the biggest shirt and shorts that could be found. She climbed into half the outfit; I climbed into the other half. We're not small gals, so these were big clothes. The residents smiled and laughed and it was so fun!"

Very proud of themselves, they decided to walk around the campus outside. "We didn't stay in step and fell into a ditch right by the highway. We could not get up! Cars would slow down, and we'd laugh harder and harder."

If you've ever been in a three-legged race, you've got a clear picture of this whole silly scene.

Janice from Minnesota didn't fall herself, thank goodness, but everything else did. While maneuvering through a crowded restaurant, Janice accidentally bumped her purse on the sneeze guard over the salad bar. "That's when the chaos began. The guard was not permanently attached, so when I bumped it, down it came along with the baskets of croutons, sunflower seeds, and so forth, that were sitting along the top. I tried grabbing the baskets as they slid past me, only to watch them explode when they hit the ground.

"The worst—and loudest—moment was when the glass guard hit the floor and shattered at my feet. Talk about a red face! I still look for my picture at the entrance along with a warning sign: DO NOT ADMIT THIS PERSON."

Bright and Creative

Sunnies are the very definition of right-brained, creative types. If there's a clever, offbeat way to solve a problem the

Sunny finds it, even at a young age. Sheena from Texas was a mere toddler when her mother put her to bed and firmly told her, "I love you, but if you get out of bed before morning, I'm going to have to spank you."

Dr. Spock hadn't considered creative Sheena.

Twenty minutes later, her mother heard the pitter-patter of little feet coming down the hall. Sheena poked her head around the corner and said, "Good morning, Mama!"

I'm not sure if the stranger in the next story was a clever Sunny or just plain strange.

Peggy from Texas was eating at a restaurant with her sister and two young children when out of nowhere a woman came up behind her and started talking in her ear like Donald Duck.

"I turned to look at her, and the stranger was gone. A few minutes later, she passed behind me and did it again. I asked my family if they'd heard her, and they cracked up—so hard, my sister almost wet her pants."

Cheer up. If the woman had walked by my table, she probably would've talked like Porky Pig, and then I'd have been forced to follow her to the salad bar and push her face in the cottage cheese!

The Brightest Star in the Sky

When Sunnies enter a room, they fill it with sunshine and laughter. And noise. Phyllis Diller's laugh was once described as the sound of an old Chevrolet starting up on a below-freezing morning.

Yes, Sunnies are loud. Sitting in bed having a conversation with Bill one night, he cut me off with, "Shh! You'll wake the kids!"

"How could I wake two sleeping children?" I demanded in a loud voice.

Oh, I see.

The Sunny's ever-performing approach to life can become tiresome for those around us who long for a few quiet, overcast days. The truth is, the Sunny needs to hide behind a few clouds from time to time. Being "on" all the time is exhausting. In some cases, the ha-ha funny side of the Sunny comes from what my friend Rosita calls "a deep need not to cry."

Joanna from Georgia says, "Humor brings me out of depression and helps me see the brighter side of a situation. Almost all clowns have a sad past."

I've used humor as a coping mechanism myself a time or two (or three or four). But it's so much better than all the other choices, don't you think? It's free, legal, clean, safe, and available twenty-four hours a day.

It's also addictive, but in the most positive sense.

Mary from Oregon is a classic Sunny: "It started out as a sunny summer's day, perfect for getting out my three-wheeler and heading off to a yard sale. My bargain of the day was a large palm plant. I plunked down my two dollars and loaded my plant in the basket in the rear of the three-wheeler, which is like a big adult tricycle."

But Mary hadn't counted on the quizzical looks and amused stares she received as she pedaled along the streets in the pouring-down rain with a very large palm plant behind her.

"One driver slowed down to gape as I was passing in the opposite direction, so I yelled out, 'Well, don't you ever water your plants?!!'"

The Sunny in Review

Favorite career:	Sales
Favorite hobby:	Spending money
Favorite sport:	Cheerleading
Favorite humor:	*Candid Camera*
Favorite clothing:	Colorful, casual

Favorite city: Phoenix (214 sunny days a year!)
Favorite magazine: *People*
Favorite color: Red
Favorite day: Saturday
Favorite season: Summer
Favorite holiday: Fourth of July
Favorite hymn: "There Is Sunshine in My Soul"
Life verse: "He who is of a merry heart has a con-
                        tinual feast" (Proverbs 15:15).

CHAPTER 17

The Cloudy Sense of Humor: On Second Thought, Take the Umbrella

One misty, moisty morning,
When cloudy was the weather . . .
—*Nursery Rhyme*

Deep is the word that comes to mind when we think of the *Cloudy* personality. A deep thinker, a deep digger for truth— and a deep well of tears from which to draw bucketfuls as needed.

The Cloudy goes to the well often, as the wettest of the four weather personalities.

Since 28 percent of us are Cloudies, how wonderful of God to create just a few more Sunnies to keep Cloudies from drowning in deep, depressing water. Of course, it works both ways. The Sunnies need the Cloudies to keep them from consuming themselves in a fiery flame of misplaced enthusiasm.

Cloudies touch a cool finger of water to our Sunny lips and say, "Calm down. Be still. Make a list."

Here's our list of eight traits that often appear on a Cloudy horizon, taking special note of the Cloudy sense of humor.

Cirrus-ly Speaking

In cloud lingo, cirrus clouds are the lofty ones, reaching for the highest of heavens, with wispy curls like angel's hair. That's our Cloudy, an angel to all who know them. Often deeply spiritual, Cloudies love nothing better than studying, researching, and seeking after truth.

They've done all five years of Bible Study Fellowship—twice. Their copy of *Vine's Expository Dictionary* is dog-eared.

The somber Maundy Thursday service is their favorite part of the Easter season (unlike their Sunny sister, who can't wait for the trumpets and ta-das of Resurrection Sunday).

The Cloudies take life seriously, as well they should. Somebody should, and the Cloudies are good at it. What they're not skilled at is giving themselves permission to laugh. The Cloudy definitely has a sense of humor—every healthy person does—but allowing that side to come out and play requires patience and encouragement from the sidelines.

Sherry from Colorado admits she needs lessons on "how to laugh at myself more often. It's so hard because I'm such a serious person." The Lord has a way of humbling us, even if only to help us develop that sense of our humor-filled humanity.

Just after her thirtieth birthday, Sherry "received a pleasant surprise. A cute guy asked me to go skiing. The fact that he had been on the ski patrol for four years during college didn't faze me, even though I'm only a beginner/intermediate skier.

"I hadn't been on a date in almost a year and was really trying to impress him. I bought a new ski suit, hat, gloves, and goggles and insisted on driving my four-wheel drive."

Impressive.

"As we were heading down the highway, I was talking so much to ease my tenseness [ooh, big step for a Cloudy!] that I didn't notice how fast I was going.

"The highway patrolman asked, 'Did you realize you were going 57 in a 50 mph zone, and at a dangerous intersection at that? Let me see your driver's license.'"

Sherry gulped and handed it over.

"Ma'am, did you know your license expired three months ago?"

No, she didn't.

"Well, Miss Dixon, I was just going to give you a warning for speeding, but because your license has expired, I'm going to write a citation for speeding. The gentleman there can drive you both home."

Steve could not drive stick shift.

Steve never called Sherry again.

She says, "All I could do was laugh at all my mishaps. Maybe perfectionists aren't always perfect."

Stratus Listus

Like the low, gray blanket known as the stratus cloud, the Cloudy covers every base, checks every detail, crosses every *t* and dots every *i*.

Cloudies actually use those daily planning guides that most of us bought with the best intentions but have yet to take out of the box. Their neat, legible handwriting covers each page with carefully thought out ideas and plans for the days, weeks, months, and years ahead.

I am a closet Cloudy, meaning when no one is looking I make lists, too, but on my computer where no one will ever stumble on them and laugh at the very notion of me trying to get that much accomplished in one day. You see, putting an enthusiastic Sunny with a Cloudy-style Day-Timer is a dangerous thing. We Sunnies fill each tiny fifteen-minute segment with tasks like "get caught up on laundry."

In fifteen minutes? Very dangerous.

The Cloudy would never do such a thing, because they are efficiency experts, having calculated exactly how long each chore will take to finish, allowing for both best and worst case scenarios.

Worst case scenarios are a Cloudy forte.

Ms. Responsible

Every family needs someone to be responsible, and the Cloudy gets the job every time. She or he keeps the calendar up to date, packs the lunches, checks the homework folder, gets the library books back on time (and probably volunteers there twice a month).

Cloudies know what it takes to make the world go around, and it's one word—*organization*. Unless the Cloudy literally writes "do something fun" on their list of "Things to Do Today," it might not happen. Cloudies genuinely want to include more fun in their lives, if only because they've read eleven articles recently on the health benefits of humor, but they aren't sure where to begin.

Gale from Kentucky works with a woman named Debbie who, if not a Cloudy, certainly jumps in to be helpful in typical Cloudy fashion. "It was a busy day at the doctor's office," Gale begins. "People were scurrying around, pulling charts, weighing patients, and making appointments.

"Debbie decided to do some filing in the huge lateral files we use to house thousands of file folders. A security feature of the file cabinets is a cable in the back that is supposed to keep more than one file drawer from opening at a time. This cabinet's cable was broken, and as luck would have it, two file drawers opened at once, which caused the entire cabinet to tip over!

"Debbie caught the cabinet and was keeping it from falling any further, but she couldn't stand it upright. The beautiful plants on top of the cabinet started sliding off. Some crashed to the floor, but one plant landed right on top of Debbie's head.

"There she stood, muscles bulging, arms shaking, with a pot on her head and soil running down her uniform."

"Helppp!" screamed Debbie.

Gale says, "I immediately sized up the situation and did what I thought seemed appropriate. I took the pot off her head."

[I'm pegging Gale as a potential Sunny at this point.]

The good news is, the rest of the office soon arrived and spared Debbie any additional cloudbursts. The nice thing about a Cloudy is, since they keep a good supply of tears handy, they can water their own plants anytime.

Rain, Rain, Go Away

I'm by no means suggesting Cloudies cry all the time, but I can safely deduce that they don't laugh enough. I know that because they tell me so. When asked on the survey, "On a scale of one to ten, how important is humor in your life?" the responses of women I'd peg to be Cloudies have similar scores—low.

Barbara from Illinois gave her need for humor a 5 and admitted, "I'm too serious, but I was born that way." While she kindly said she enjoyed my particular stories, she insisted, "I hate slapstick."

Yep. Cloudies hate physical comedy. Too demeaning. While Sunnies are hooting in the corner at some poor creature who has tripped over a string in the carpet, the Cloudy glares at her

Sunny sisters, hissing, "How can you laugh at that man? You're so rude!" Then the Cloudy assists the befuddled soul while the Sunnies are sliding down the wall with breathless laughter.

Emilie from California also rated humor a low 5 and confessed, "I need help!" Susan from France only gave it a 3 and explained, "The books I go for are novels or self-help. I'm just not very funny." Patti from Ohio showed a little more propensity for humor, giving it a 6 and agreed, "I want to enjoy life but not be outrageous."

Oh, the self-control of a Cloudy! I love being outrageous, and in fact have little choice in the matter. So it is for the Cloudy and their subdued approach to humor. They definitely see the value of it and don't mind the occasional chuckle, as long as there is absolutely no chance of their being seen as ridiculous, outrageous, foolish, or any other credibility-reducing term.

Changeable Skies

As list-making and organized as Cloudies may be, they also can be moody and unpredictable. Those fluffy cumulus clouds can, without warning, turn into cirrocumulus clouds, a sign of unsettled weather. Authors and artists are often Cloudies, because of their attention to detail, and their temperaments are legendary.

Cloudies may just be having a bad day.

Or they may have spent the afternoon at the dentist.

Mary Ann from Texas had observers trying to figure out what sort of mood she was in after "a long drawn-out affair with my dentist (don't panic). The unexpectedly lengthy tryst left me numb and drooling as I paid the bill.

"On the way home I stopped at the grocery store and reached into my shoulder bag. My change purse popped open and coins spilled all over the floor. A silver-haired gent standing behind me chuckled and said to his younger companion, 'Look at that! Quick, grab as many as you can!'"

They handed over the errant coins, and Mary Ann nodded a polite thanks, not trusting her drooling lips to function. She spied candy bars on a nearby shelf and took two.

Moments later, the cashier said, "That'll be eighty-six cents."

Puzzled, Mary Ann murmured, "That can't be right. You only charged me for the vinegar."

"But that's all that's here. See?"

Thoroughly confused, Mary Ann groped in her purse for money and discovered the two candy bars. Muttering a slobbery apology, she handed the candy over to the cashier while her silver-haired observer laughed out loud, saying "You think that's bad. You should see her work Kmart!"

The Early Cloud Gets the Best Corner of the Sky

This will seem to be a contradiction, but though their moods may be mercurial, their habits are as predictable as the phases of the moon. Cloudies are always punctual. Always. Early, in fact. They don't want to miss anything, nor draw attention to themselves by arriving late (unlike Sunnies, who love it when every eye in the room follows their late entrance).

Cloudies may appear aloof, cool, and distant, but don't you believe it. Mostly, they're shy, waiting for someone to draw them out. Since they are ultra-considerate of the feelings of others and are highly-sensitive in nature, they will wait patiently for someone to notice them rather than wave their arms and shout, "I'm here!"

Lois from Wisconsin shares the old story of an attractive young widow who visited a new church. The pastor met her at the door and made a real effort to help her feel welcome. He went on and on, saying, "We're so happy that you came to visit us. In fact, why don't you choose three hymns today?"

The young widow was overwhelmed with the pastor's generous offer. She promptly strolled into the church, looked over the congregation, turned to the pastor, and pointed: "I'll take him and him and him!"

Whine-o-Metric Pressure

Henri Bergson said it best: "Laughter is the corrective force which prevents us from becoming cranks."

Moody Cloudies can get cranky, but the truth is, they are perfectionists, and life is not perfect, so—bless them—they whine about it. Georgia from Ohio was "getting impatient with my super-picky husband and blurted out, 'Boy, are you a perfectionist!'

"He retorted, 'I married you, didn't I?'"

They have definite ideas of right and wrong, not just in the larger moral sense, but in teeny tiny ways. For the Cloudy, there is a right way to do everything. A right way to attach stamps to envelopes (in the right corner, equidistant from both edges), a correct way to mix frozen orange juice (run warm water over the can first), a definite method for peeling apples (stem to bottom, peel all in one piece).

During break time at a writing seminar I attended, I hunted through the basket filled with tea bags, checking out the different flavors, and was amazed to find all my four weather personalities represented there!

For the Sunny, there was a shiny, bright-yellow packet of tea called "I Love Lemon."

For the Stormy, there was an exotic foreign tea marked "strong, robust flavor."

For the Foggy, there was a pitiful little tea sack—no colorful wrapper, no name, not even a string or a tag.

For the Cloudy—ahh! Lipton Tea, the Choicest Blend, the most dependable of all, with directions on the back "for the perfect cup of tea."

Even the small flap directed one to "pull up gently."

A Cloudy wouldn't think of doing it any other way.

Altitudinous and Cerebral

So what does the head-in-the-clouds man or woman find funny? Does any sort of humor appeal to the Cloudy?

Most definitely, it's cerebral humor. Clever wordplays, puns, and humorous material that makes you think, causes you to pause, or draws on references from literature and the arts.

Or, is just plain quick.

Lee Ann from New Mexico was watching an *Oprah* episode about people's preferences, such as which way they like the toilet paper roll to go.

She asked her brother-in-law, "Are you a sock-sock-shoe-shoe person or a sock-shoe-sock-shoe?"

After thinking about it a few seconds, he decided, "I could go either way."

Lee Ann quipped, "I guess that makes you bisoxual!"

A pun is the lowest form of humor—when you don't think of it first.

—Oscar Levant

And when the Cloudy laughs, it's a garden hose sound—*ssss*. A little bit leaking out at a time. No braying donkeys or howling wolves for this personality. Not hardly. It will be done in good taste, only when and where appropriate, and not at all if one might risk offending another.

Perfectionist Cloudies usually marry loosey-goosey Sunnies, which makes things interesting.

Sally's grandfather was minister of a large Presbyterian church in Denver, Colorado. "Shortly after he became the pastor, he announced that he and his wife would soon have a blessed event with the birth of their second child. All the women of the congregation were anxious to see the baby as soon as it was born.

"Now there is no such thing as an ugly baby, but when that child was born a few months later, he came pretty close. He was tall and thin, bright red, wrinkled up, and totally bald.

"According to family history, my grandmother exclaimed, 'My goodness, how can I show off this baby to all the ladies at church?'"

After thinking things over for a minute, Sally's look-on-the-bright-side grandfather replied, "Well, I guess you'll just have to show them his feet."

The Cloudy in Review

Favorite career:	Library science
Favorite hobby:	Balancing checkbook
Favorite sport:	Chess
Favorite humor:	*Prairie Home Companion*
Favorite clothing:	Coordinated, conservative
Favorite city:	Buffalo, New York (206 cloudy days a year!)
Favorite magazine:	*Architectural Digest*
Favorite color:	Blue
Favorite day:	Sunday
Favorite season:	Fall
Favorite holiday:	Memorial Day
Favorite hymn:	"Rescue the Perishing"
Life verse:	"Sorrow is better than laughter. For by a sad countenance the heart is made better." (Ecclesiastes 7:3)

CHAPTER 18

✿

The Stormy Sense of Humor: It Was a Dark and Stormy Night

Hello! We heard you at the door, but just thought you were part of the bad weather.
—Arthur Baer

With a label like *Stormy*, it's clear we're in for some intense weather! Take shelter in a dry, warm place while we meet the coldest of the four weather personalities. Not to suggest Stormies are heartless and cruel, but they do have the ability to remain more detached than the other three temperaments. And like a cold blast of air, they make a dramatic entrance.

I meet Stormies everywhere I go. If there are sixteen million thunderstorms a year all over the planet, no wonder there's a good bit of thunder and lightning happening under our roofs. Our own informal research here rings true to me: 23 percent of Stormies sounds just right.

And right is what Stormies want to be. I'm a fairly even mix of Sunny and Stormy, so I know this one well. Stand back and observe eight traits of the Stormy weather personality—from a safe distance!

Explosive and Strong-Willed

From the Stormy's point of view, there is one way—their way. Like the bumper sticker says, MY WAY OR THE HIGHWAY.

Stormies have an answer for everything, even if they've never thought about it before. Rather than say, "I don't know," they will make stuff up and then, if necessary, alter history to make certain that the day they made that statement, it was accurate based on the information you gave them.

We Stormies insist "the buck stops here," but in truth, if we can pass the buck and blame someone else, we're even happier.

That's why it's always a good giggle when a Stormy is involved in something where they can't exert their strong will and get the job done. For example, Cathy's husband returned from buying diapers without a coupon (ouch), and announced that it was time to potty train their two-year-old son, Jacob, right now.

"Jacob is too young for this," Cathy patiently explained. "He doesn't have a clue what to do with a potty."

Naturally, this became a challenge for Stormy hubby, who marched into the bathroom, Jacob in tow. Cathy, meanwhile, was outside the room, on her knees, with her ear pressed firmly against the keyhole.

Hubby David discussed the potty and paper with Jacob in typical, no-nonsense fashion. Cathy must have collapsed when David suddenly said authoritatively, "Jake, that is not a hat."

Lightning Leader

In weather words, when a flash of lightning occurs, a *leader* stroke zigzags to the ground, forming a narrow path for the *return* stroke to race back up. How like our Stormy leader, who, in a stroke of energy and decisive action, clears the path for others to follow—whether they want to or not.

Brigadier General Wilma Vaught once admitted, "What I wanted to be when I grew up was—in charge." Go, Wilma. A classic Stormy, as are many military leaders. They command attention, they inspire confidence, and when necessary they pull rank.

Stormies are natural leaders. They walk into any small group and, within fifteen minutes, nominate themselves president. There wasn't an election or anything, they just stood up, pounded the table, and said, "All right, here's what we're going to do."

All heads nodded. "Okay."

Once again, the Stormy sensed the leadership void and filled it. Admirably. Or is that Majorly? Generally? Captainly? You get the idea. The Stormy is in charge.

Decision-making is one of the key distinctives of the Stormy. A television reporter once interviewed a famous Stormy person . . .

Reporter: To what do you attribute your success?
Stormy: Two words: Right decisions.

Reporter: But how did you make those decisions?
Stormy: One word: Experience.
Reporter: But how did you get that experience?!
Stormy: Two words: Wrong decisions.

We Stormies climb the ladder of success wrong by wrong, learning by our mistakes, hoping no one notices, then moving up the next wrong, uh, rung.

Dangerous Business

Stormies love taking risks. They thrive on it, draw energy from it. While a Cloudy might take a walk in the rain, enjoying the gentle caress of each little drop, a Stormy thinks a stroll through a thunderstorm is more interesting. Their sense of invincibility gives them courage—or makes them fools. Either way, when risk is involved, the Stormy is the one who won't shrink back.

Gale was a thrill seeker from an early age. She would climb up their big mulberry tree to get to the roof of their chicken coop and curl up with a good book. "One day, after reading about some adventurers who had rappelled down a mountain, I decided I would try to recreate the experience. I tied one end of a rope to the tree limb and the other end of the rope in a slipknot around my waist.

"I positioned myself on the edge of the sloping roof and jumped off. Seconds later I found myself lying on the ground wondering where I'd gone wrong. In my haste to have the perfect jump, I'd failed to consider the fact that the shed was twelve feet tall and my rope was forty feet long. Miraculously, I only suffered a few bruises. Back to the drawing board."

Stormy children: Do not try this at home! Honor thy mother and thy father!

Since laughing out loud is, in a sense, its own kind of risk, is it any surprise that when the Stormy finally cuts loose, it's one big blast—*ppaaahhh!* Like the fire siren at noon, the Stormy laugh cuts through the atmosphere with deafening sound and with about the same frequency—once a day.

Stormies don't laugh often or easily. They wait impatiently, arms folded over their chest, until something worthy of their response is offered. Make-me-laugh is the look on their faces. This-better-be-good is the body language that goes with it.

That's why it's so fun when Stormies do laugh. Like ball lightning, it's a rare occurrence, worthy of the record books. And, like thunder, it roars through the room and can, in fact, be heard ten miles away.

Since Stormies truly don't care what others think of them, when they're ready to laugh, they do so, whether anyone else is willing to come along for the ride or not. Flying on a plane (how else would I do it?), I was reading something funny, came to the punch line, and let out a laugh blaster. *Pah!* All the people in the aisle seats turned around. What-did-they-put-in-her-roasted-peanuts? was the look on their faces.

Tornadic Activity

Tornadoes are not uncommon in our part of the country, and smart people pay attention when the forecasters say to take cover.

Unfortunately, Stormies don't always broadcast tornado warnings. They simply spin into a room, tossing debris everywhere, and then leave in a huff. When it comes to addressing the volatile issue of our tendency to get angry, we Stormies sometimes justify our behavior by saying, "Sure, I get mad, but it blows over in two minutes."

Right. So does a tornado, but look at what a mess it leaves behind. Will Rogers must have known a Stormy or two when he wrote, "People who fly into a rage always make a bad landing."

Gretchen from Washington deals with a double dose of this at her house. She admits, "My youngest son, Josh, has a temper like his mama—short and difficult to control. One day when he was in the first grade, he brought home a teacher's note saying he had been in trouble several times that week for letting his temper get the best of him.

"I gave Josh a lecture on controlling anger, and decided to show a little empathy. I told him I understood his problem and that his temper was inherited from me—it was in my genes. Later, my husband mentioned the note to Josh and reminded him to keep his anger in check. Josh said, 'Don't worry, Daddy, it's Mama's fault. I only lose my temper when she wears a hairnet and jeans!'"

Sheryl from Oklahoma understands why a Stormy needs humor: "It's God's pressure valve in my life. If I don't get enough laughter, I blow a gasket."

Endless Energy

Ask a Stormy what they do in their spare time, and watch their face go blank. Spare time? What's that? Do you mean when I'm sleeping?

Stormies pride themselves on not requiring much shut-eye, insisting that five or six hours a night is all they need, with a "power nap" or two thrown in for good measure.

Work is what makes the Stormy tick, which explains why they see little need for humor in their lives. How productive is that? they wonder, reaching for another stack of correspondence. Let's have a meeting instead. Taking a laughter break is actually very productive, sending you back to your task with renewed energy, a fresh outlook on things, and increased creative potential. Those things aren't quite bottom-line enough for Stormies, who think Big Picture and skip the details, leaving those for their super-efficient Cloudy administrative assistants.

If you are a Stormy and are still unconvinced about the many benefits of humor, here's an angle you'll understand: Funny means money. The most successful managers are those who create a workplace where fun is part of the strategic mix. It builds loyalty among both employees and customers, reduces stress and all the medical costs that go with it, and lines you up for an even bigger promotion.

See? I knew you'd see it my way.

No Waiting

If you want to humor a Stormy, make it snappy. Literally. Short, to-the-point stories, jokes, and one-liners are the way to reach a Stormy's funny bone, well-hidden inside his or her expensive tailored suit. Get-to-the-punch-line! their eyes will say. Time is money for the Stormy, and long, drawn-out stories cost too much.

Impatient Stormies often marry ultra-patient Foggies (more on that in the next chapter). My Bill has his own ways of handling his impatient wife. When we pull into a parking lot, Bill sighs, "Why don't you go ahead and tell me where to park, I know you've already spotted the space you want."

Smart guy.

Polly from Georgia confesses, "Impatience was my middle name. My husband, Dave, moved at his own pace, but I wanted him to walk faster, especially when it came to cutting the grass."

The mower wasn't repaired and the grass grew, along with her impatience. Finally she prayed that the Lord would motivate Dave, "because I can't." She promised God, "I'll be patient even if the grass grows above my knees"—and it almost did!

One morning their dog began barking, and her husband said in amazement, "There are cows in the yard!"

They had no idea where they came from. Polly begged her husband to get them out of their yard, to which Dave responded, "No, let's wait until they eat the grass."

Not in the mood for a roundup, Polly and Dave located the owner and found out the cows had smelled the grass from a mile away.

Polly says, "Our mower is broken again, but I'll be patient because I don't know who the Lord might send to cut the grass this time!"

Right as Rain

With their traits of always being right, being decisive, and being in charge, Stormies are also always happy to tell you what to do.

Just ask them.

On second thought, you won't have to.

JoAnn from New York remembers the days before children (B.C.), when she'd join her husband for Sunday breakfast at different restaurants. On one occasion, her husband asked his usual question, "What are you getting to eat?"

"A ham-and-cheese omelette."

"You always order the same thing," he said, exasperated.

"I love ham-and-cheese omelettes, and that's what I'm ordering," she insisted.

"But we need to try different things, expand our horizons," he grumbled. With that, he ordered the corn pancakes.

Imagine their surprise when the waitress appeared with a plate with two pancakes on it and a can of whole kernel corn dumped on the top! "When I saw the look on my husband's face, I laughed so hard that I had tears rolling down my cheeks. Every time he took a bite I would start laughing again. The joke was on me when I literally choked on a piece of ham that was in my omelette!"

More than one Stormy has had to eat *crow* when they make a mistake, but eat *corn*?

Taking Charge

Even though they may not have their sense of humor ever at the ready, the Stormy is definitely the one to call when an emergency strikes.

Myra Caye's emergency was really off the wall. Or rather, *in* the wall. Her puppy had climbed out of his crate, terrorized her utility room, jumped on top of the dryer, knocked down the vent, and tried to wiggle through the four-inch hole in the wall, which he managed to do—halfway.

In Myra's words, "The outside of my house looked like a live trophy wall. As the pup tried to free himself, he would literally spin on the wall!

"I tried to stuff him back, but no such luck. I then called 911 and requested help from the fire department. They arrived, and the life squad pulled into my driveway, creating quite a stir in my neighborhood. They tried soapy water, but the dog was stuck fast."

She tried to use a hammer and screwdriver to remove a brick from the house to free the dog, "but every time I struck the screwdriver the dog licked my hand, and I was afraid I'd miss and hit him in the head."

Two hours went by, with many pleas for help directed at various authorities, but no remedy. Frantic, she called a vet who agreed to give her a tranquilizer for the dog, if she would drive the thirty miles to get it. Finally at 9:30 P.M., the puppy swallowed the pill, and by 10:00 he was very relaxed. It took an adult supporting the puppy on each end, one inside, one outside, a chief with a chisel, and lots of soap to get this puppy out of the wall.

The moral of this story is: When life is driving you up the wall, call Myra Caye!

The Stormy in Review

Favorite career:	CEO
Favorite hobby:	Darts
Favorite sport:	Ice hockey

Favorite humor:	*Rowan and Martin's Laugh-In* (Even super-Stormy Richard Nixon said, "Sock it to me!")
Favorite clothing:	Suits
Favorite city:	Biloxi (94 storms and 7 hurricanes a year)
Favorite magazine:	*Forbes*
Favorite color:	Black
Favorite day:	Monday
Favorite season:	Winter
Favorite holiday:	Labor Day
Favorite hymn:	"How Firm a Foundation"
Life verse:	"In all labor there is profit, But idle chatter leads only to poverty." (Proverbs 14:23)

CHAPTER 19

The Foggy Sense of Humor: It Was a Gray and Foggy Day

He was so benevolent, so merciful a man that he would have held an umbrella over a duck in a shower of rain.
—*Douglas Jerrold*

When I tell you the *Foggy* is the driest of the four weather personalities, you might protest, "But, Liz! Fog is damp, not dry." We're speaking more of wit than weather here. The Foggies have a dry, droll sense of humor that permeates their entire outlook on life. More observer than participant, the Foggy offers a thoughtful response amidst the climatic chaos of the overly enthusiastic Sunny, the oversensitive Cloudy, and the overpowering Stormy.

Foggies are never *over*, they're *under*. Under the covers, under the weather, or under the influence of a strong-willed Stormy boss, spouse, or parent. Our surveys of women pegged the Foggies at 17 percent of the population. Prepare for some fun in the fog with my favorite of the four weather personalities. Of their many touted traits, we'll look at eight.

Well Grounded

Fog hovers near the ground, or rises from the sea when warm air meets cool water on a calm night and collects at the surface. So it is with the Foggy temperament, which is laid back, cool, calm, and collected.

The Sunny and Stormy will both consider the Foggy dull, but that's neither fair nor accurate. Foggies are just quiet, without any desire to draw attention to themselves. Growing up in an all Sunny/Stormy family, I don't remember even meeting a Foggy until I met my wonderful Bill. Okay, maybe I met some and didn't notice. Or, didn't appreciate their finer points.

Then, in my early thirties, I met my future husband and was introduced to the joys of Foggyhood. He is low-key and easygoing, and nothing ruffles his feathers—except me when I'm on a Stormy tirade.

Foggies are steady, predictable, dependable. If Bill says he will meet me at the airport at a certain time, he's there. Not early, mind you, like the Cloudy who always worries, nor late like the Sunny who has a million excuses, nor absent like the

Stormy who would suggest a cab. The Foggy is simply there and waiting.

Will a Foggy be happy to see you? Of course. But don't expect balloons and streamers and a big WELCOME HOME sign. Foggies enjoy parties where they can sit in a corner and watch everyone else, but they aren't likely to throw the party. (They're happy to stay until the end and help clean up, bless them, if you'll just tell them where to put the plates.)

Not only might Foggies forget to bring the confetti, they might also forget to shout, "Ya-hoo!" Early in our marriage, I was all wound up about something while Bill just stared and nodded every few minutes with no change of expression whatsoever. Finally, I paused for breath and blurted out in exasperation, "Just once, I wish you'd get excited!"

His face was utterly blank, his voice flat: "But I am excited."

okeydokey

On our first shopping expedition together, I saw my Foggy Bill's agreeable personality in action when I held up a textured sweater I was sure he'd enjoy wearing.

"Whadya think of this, honey?"

He shrugged. "That's okay."

"Oh!" I stuffed it back in the pile, posthaste.

Obviously he hated it. In my family, "That's okay" was a code phrase for "That's the most abhorrent thing I've ever laid eyes on. Get rid of it immediately before I faint dead away."

I chose another sweater, this one in subdued stripes, quite different from the first. "How 'bout this one, sweetie?"

He shrugged. "That's okay."

Oh, no! The man was apparently more difficult to please than I'd first thought. I gulped and ditched the second choice in favor of a classic solid that was sure to suit any man.

"Isn't this one nice?" I asked in my tentative-new-bride voice.

He shrugged. "That's okay."

A pattern was forming, and not on the sweaters. I worked my way along the shelves and amassed another dozen more "that's okay" responses before I tossed the last sweater in the air in frustration and whined, "I've run out of options, Bill. Don't you like any of these?"

"No, I like all of them," he insisted.

"But you said they're just *okay*."

"Right."

"Which means . . ."

He shrugged. "It means they're okay. I like them."

"You like them all equally well?!"

What a concept for an opinionated Stormy to grasp!

The man is sooo agreeable. He eats my cooking, he puts up with my grousing, he humors my need for variety when he would be perfectly content eating cinnamon Pop-Tarts for breakfast every day for the rest of his life.

When it comes to amusing Foggies, there are many avenues to choose from, as long as you don't require them to laugh out loud. They'll take the time needed to absorb the cerebral humor of a Woody Allen, yet smile at the quick sight gags of the Marx Brothers too.

Cartoons like *Dilbert* are popular with Foggies because (1) Dilbert is a computer engineering geek and (2) the scenarios reflect workplace humor with hysterical accuracy and (3) they take ten seconds to read, leaving plenty of time for lunch, a nap, etc.

In an effort to be agreeable, Foggies may make assumptions rather than ask questions, which leads to interesting aha! moments. Renee from Florida rented a room in the home of a sweet, elderly lady. "We shared the kitchen and bathroom, which worked out just fine."

She continues, "As our friendship grew, I took on several household tasks to aid my older friend. One morning I was feeling particularly industrious and decided to clean out the bathroom. Never able to find a brush to scrub the toilet, I'd always used a sponge, but since I was about to use a strong new cleaner, I asked if she had a toilet-cleaning brush in the house."

Renee's aha! moment had arrived.

"It's hanging in the shower next to the shower cap and other accessories," the older woman explained.

All those months, Renee had been using that brush as a back-scrubber during her shower.

Was Job a Foggy?

The phrase *patience of Job* fits the Foggy like a moist cloud of air wraps itself around a lighthouse. If we're sitting at a red light and Bill is driving, I'm on the passenger side with an imaginary gas pedal, foot poised, eyes darting back and forth, ready to take off the minute the light changes.

When it does and we don't immediately take off, I realize he just didn't see it.

"Bill. It's green."

He's doing what all Foggies do at red lights: Keeping his hands at ten o'clock and two o'clock and staring at the dashboard. I realize he just didn't hear me.

"Bill. It's green."

He turns to me and says, "There'll be another one."

Sure, in the next millenium, but I didn't want to wait that long. Foggies are wonderful at waiting. And waiting.

Blessed Are the Peacemakers

Foggies have an exceptional ability to calm people down by seeing both sides of an argument and helping the two opponents get together for a truce. Consequently, they make wonderful negotiators and business meeting facilitators.

When tempers flare at work, sending Cloudies off to the ladies' room crying, Stormies stamping off for a caffeine fix, and

Sunnies looking desperately for a funny story to tell to break the tension, the Foggy moves in on little cat's feet, cooling the temperature of the room and, like fog, confusing everyone.

"What were we so upset about?"

"I don't know, I can't even see the problem anymore."

"Will you help me? I am totally turned around here."

It's a purposeful wet blanket, this fog. While it can sometimes dampen enthusiasm, more often it acts as a calming influence at work and at home.

Even in their desire for peace, the Foggies can toss in a few surprises of their own. Cindy from Illinois was amazed when her Sunday school class threw a surprise birthday party for her, and her "shy, stable, but not boring husband" assembled a whole bag of goodies for her "twilight" years. "Things like batteries to keep me charged and sticky-note pads to help me remember things.

"It was special because it was so out of character for my quiet husband to put together something so utterly funny. He doesn't like surprises but knows I love them."

Stubborn as a Rule

The couple next to me on the plane were having a discussion that was so typically *Foggy v. Stormy* that I had to concentrate on the latch of the overhead compartment to keep my composure.

Stormy-she says, "Here, honey, try this mocha-bunga-java coffee. It's delicious."

Foggy-he replies, "No, thanks."

She holds it out to him. "C'mon, try it. You'll love it."

He shakes his head. "I really don't like those tricky coffees."

"You'll like this one," she persists, holding it closer.

"I'll pass."

She now has it right under his nose. "Just one taste!"

"No, thanks," he insists, shaking his head.

"Trust me, this is too good to miss," she says through clenched teeth, getting almost as hot as the coffee.

"I don't want any."

"One taste!" She is pressing the cup against his lips.

He remains cool but stubborn. "I'd rather not."

I clocked it. This went on for seven minutes. We'd flown over an entire state, and they were still going on about the coffee. What was the problem? Stormies are stubborn—but Foggies are even more stubborn. They dig in their heels, and it's all over.

(The people-pleasing Sunny in me almost jumped in and said, "Here, I'll be happy to try it!")

Indecisive? Are You Sure?

Stubborn on occasion, yes. Indecisive, always. If you ask a Foggy, "Do you have trouble making decisions?" they'll consider it for a very long time, stammering and stuttering toward a response.

"Well . . . um . . . gee . . . uh . . . yes and no."

Karen from Nevada admits, "Here is how indecisive I am. I was changing planes in the airport and stopped by the gift shop for something to read. I couldn't decide what to get—a newspaper or a book. Hmm. One book was entitled *How to Overcome Indecisiveness*. I couldn't decide if I should buy it or not and stood there debating about it for ten minutes, back and forth, back and forth.

"Finally I decided not to get it, but by the time I got on board my next flight, I wished I'd bought it."

Wit Served Dry, Shaken Not Stirred

Foggies almost never laugh out loud, but they smile all the time. So much so, you wonder what they know that you don't. Sheri might be a Foggy, since she confesses, "I enjoy humor, but it takes a lot to make me laugh out loud." And Sandra from California says, "I don't laugh often—I smile out loud."

They have a wit that's as dry as fog is moist. We've all heard of a dry wit, but is there such a thing as a *wet* wit? For the Foggy, their favorite form of humor is the harmless practical joke. It fits their sense of time and energy economy to perfection: (1) You can take all the time you want to come up with the prank, pressure free, and (2) once you've pulled it off, you can get years of mileage from it by saying, "Remember the time when . . .?"

I'll bet Jean from Tennessee has enjoyed this memory again and again. "For my brother's fiftieth birthday, I sent notes to friends in different states requesting their help in pulling off a practical joke. I enclosed a birthday card with a stamped envelope and asked them to write a greeting and sign the card with their first name only, address the envelope in their handwriting and mail it well before my brother's birthday."

Then she called him on his big day, and let him ramble on about his apparent memory loss.

"Jean, I received cards from people I don't remember ever meeting," he told her.

"Really?"

"I even got a phone message from a woman named Maggie, who said she'd wait until I came to New York to celebrate my birthday! Jean, I don't know any Maggies."

Jean's inability to speak at this point let him know that she was the culprit. "He was relieved to learn that memory loss doesn't necessarily happen at fifty."

Foggies just love those "Gotchas!"

Jan from Rhode Island tells us, "My dad was a real prankster, and the five of us kids always had to be on the lookout. One evening we were all gathered in the living room when Dad headed to the kitchen. We heard the silverware drawer open and dishes being clanged around. My sister, Elaine, assumed Dad was dishing ice cream and hollered, "I'll have some too."

Dad yelled back from the kitchen, "Okay." He returned to the living room with a dish and gave it to Elaine.

She took a bite and started yelling. "This is awful! What is it?"

Jan explains, "Dad never told us he was feeding the dog. He simply gave Elaine 'some too'!"

Absentminded Professors, Lawyers, Doctors, Indian Chiefs

Foggies never outgrow their delight in such antics, but it's bad form to grow forgetful right in the middle of your own practical joke.

Pat from Indiana shares this story about her parents, now in their seventies. They had a bumper sticker on their refrigerator that read I'M SPENDING MY CHILDREN'S INHERITANCE. One day, unbeknownst to her mother, her father attached the sticker to his wife's trousers—"you guessed it, right on her 'bumper'!"

My, weren't we feeling playful? He soon forgot all about it and wandered downstairs to his workshop.

Pat explains, "An hour later, he came upstairs to find my mom putting away groceries. She had gone up and down the aisles of Winn-Dixie, a store where she knows everyone, wearing the bumper sticker firmly attached to her derriere! She can laugh about it now, but at the time I do believe she threw a package of frozen lima beans at Dad when he shamefacedly confessed what he had done."

Whether sharing a practical joke or a bit of dry wit, the Foggies value humor as much as the rest of us do. Lisa from Virginia says, "Humor has been like a lighthouse to me. Life occasionally gets dark, dreary, and full of stress, like being adrift on the ocean in the middle of the night. Humorous stories can often shed some light and relieve those stresses that bind us.

Humor can also keep us from running aground! Like a beacon in the night, humor offers hope."

The Foggy in Review

Favorite career:	Computer programming
Favorite hobby:	Taking a nap
Favorite sport:	Televised bowling
Favorite humor:	*The Bob Newhart Show*
Favorite clothing:	Jeans, sweats
Favorite city:	San Francisco
Favorite magazine:	*PC World*
Favorite color:	Gray
Favorite day:	Wednesday
Favorite season:	Spring (no snow, no mow, no leaves)
Favorite holiday:	Groundhog Day
Favorite hymn:	"It Is Well with My Soul"
Life verse:	"And having food and clothing, with these we shall be content" (1 Timothy 6:8).

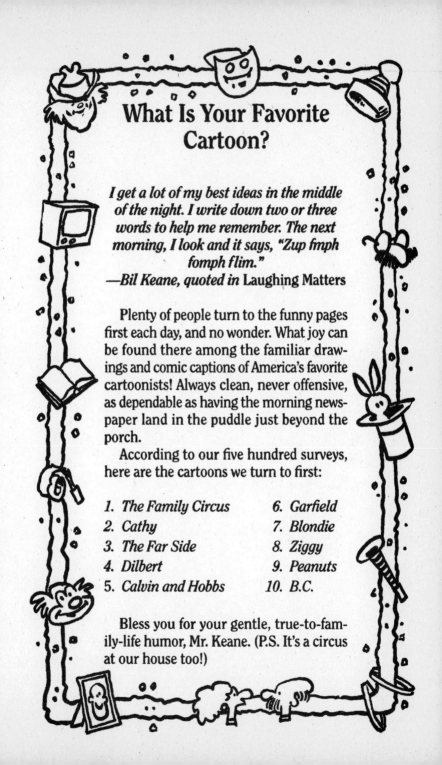

What Is Your Favorite Cartoon?

I get a lot of my best ideas in the middle of the night. I write down two or three words to help me remember. The next morning, I look and it says, "Zup fmph fomph flim."
—*Bil Keane, quoted in* Laughing Matters

Plenty of people turn to the funny pages first each day, and no wonder. What joy can be found there among the familiar drawings and comic captions of America's favorite cartoonists! Always clean, never offensive, as dependable as having the morning newspaper land in the puddle just beyond the porch.

According to our five hundred surveys, here are the cartoons we turn to first:

1. *The Family Circus*
2. *Cathy*
3. *The Far Side*
4. *Dilbert*
5. *Calvin and Hobbs*
6. *Garfield*
7. *Blondie*
8. *Ziggy*
9. *Peanuts*
10. *B.C.*

Bless you for your gentle, true-to-family-life humor, Mr. Keane. (P.S. It's a circus at our house too!)

PART FIVE

Humor and Health

I had a speech in Louisville one chilly Saturday in January. After a whole week of snow, sleet, rain, snow, sleet, rain, the parking lots in town were covered with *snirt*—snow and dirt. Underneath the snirt was *sneet*—snow and sleet, and underneath the sneet was a thin layer of ice, which you couldn't see for all the snirt and the sneet.

In typical Sunny fashion, I arrived late, sliding into the parking lot mere minutes before the opening remarks. I leaped out of the car and grabbed my purse, along with the handouts I'd brought to make the Cloudies happy. I didn't get two feet before I hit a patch of ice hiding underneath the snirt and the sneet, and went sailing across the ice, first in vertical, then horizontal, fashion.

Since Sunnies never zip our purses, the contents went flying everywhere, soon followed by my handouts—paper and snirt are a bad combination. Lying there on the ice, stunned senseless, I contemplated my best options for standing up.

Then from across the parking lot came the voice of an angel, wearing the uniform of a maintenance man. "Are you okay?" he called across the snowy parking lot.

"No, I'm not!" I moaned, assessing the damage while he made his way toward me.

I'd not torn my dress or ruined my hose, and I

had only a few spots of snirt and sneet to brush away. So far so good. But when the kind man helped me get up (I'll spare you the horrid details), I discovered that everything hurt down the left side, from shoulder to ankle. I'd hit that snirty pavement harder than I realized and was now in pretty severe pain, feeling bruises already in the making.

I had no choice. I had to speak. With my angel's guidance, I carefully hobbled across the snirt, brushed myself off, and headed for the front of the auditorium, wincing with every step.

"So glad to be with you this morning!" I said with my lips, but the rest of my body was giving a whole different message. I was listing to the left, only gestured with my right hand, and wondered how I'd make it through the hour-long presentation.

Then an amazing thing happened. They started laughing, on cue, which made me laugh. They laughed, I laughed, and sixty minutes later, nothing hurt! Thanks to the adrenaline flow that always begins when I hit the platform, and an endorphin or two that made an appearance, I had almost no pain at all. I was so excited I ran out in the parking lot and almost fell down again.

When I got home, I exclaimed, "Bill! I thought I hurt myself and I didn't!"

Sure. Until an hour later, when the adrenaline wore off. Yet, I believe the laughter bought me some grief relief, since as Carly Simon sang, "I haven't got time for the pain."

CHAPTER 20

❧

Humor and Your Body: What's Up, Doc?

One of the hardest things for any man to do is to fall down on the ice and then get up and praise the Lord.
—Josh Billings

Laughter puts the body in a state of relaxation. Think of it as "Kansas" for your constitution—nothing but gentle, green fields as far as the mind can see. In that physically relaxed state, we take our foot off the pain accelerator and put on the brake—which is the first of seven reasons why I think our bodies were built for laughter:

1. Laughter Is a Natural Pain Reducer

Our bodies were created by an amazing God who knew that we'd get broken and bruised on occasion and would need all the natural painkillers we could get our hands on.

I had a dear woman show up at a presentation in Michigan the very week I was working on this chapter. "Liz, I almost didn't come tonight because I'm in such pain."

"I am so sorry," I assured her, reaching for her hand. "What hurts?"

"Everything. That's why I decided to come. I've heard you before and know how much better I'll feel after all the laughter."

I kept my eye on her during the program and was so thrilled to watch her bending over with laughter, joy beaming from her face. Praise God for his gift of laughter. The only thing it has in common with man's answer to painkillers is, it *is* addictive!

Maybe we could be *joy junkies*!

Karla awoke early one morning to the sound of ice pelting the window. "I was a PBX operator at a department store. If one person had to report to work, it was me, if only to field all the calls from employees saying they couldn't make it in."

She went outside to catch the bus to work, "and a trip that normally took twenty minutes took twice as long. When the bus slid to a stop in front of the store, I asked the driver to please wait until I got on the sidewalk before he started off.

"I stepped down to the ground, and the cane I was using slipped, hooked my foot, and down I went—under the bus."

"Where did you go?" the worried driver called out.

"I'm under the bus," she yelled back.

"You're where?"

"Under the bus!"

"What are you doing there?"

"I'm checking your brakes!"

The good news is, Karla wasn't hurt, "just very embarrassed."

2. Laughter Increases Our Ability to Cope with Pain

If we can't make pain go away, then we can handle it better with humor. It's been said that laughter can increase our threshold of pain as much as 21 percent. Incredible. This calls for some adjustments in those prepared childbirth classes, where their suggested method for coping with pain is to breathe.

Breathe?!

I already breathe several times a day. Every chance I get, in fact. Yet they want us to face the worst voluntary pain in a woman's life—pain that our bodies spend nine months preparing for and our heads spend six intense weeks studying about—this kind of pain is handled by women breathing, women who take an aspirin for a tiny twitch over their left eye?

I practiced my breathing all six weeks, but remained unconvinced.

When the big day came and I went into labor, I dutifully breathed for twelve hours.

"What do you need?" my coach, Bill, asked, sweating profusely. He was breathing, too, but it wasn't cutting the pain one iota.

"Something funny!" I gasped.

Bill rummaged around in the big bag of tricks we'd brought to the hospital with us and came up with Dave Barry's funny book *Babies and Other Hazards of Sex*, the subtitle of which is *How to Make a Tiny Person in Nine Months with Tools You Probably Have Around the Home*.

We were breathing, praying, and laughing, breathing, praying, and laughing until we reached the twenty-sixth hour of labor, at which point all three nursing shifts had come and gone and the first group was back.

"She's still here!" they sang out.

I was singing a happy tune as well when my anesthesiologist, the doctor with the drugs, came in with a big button that said JUST SAY YES TO DRUGS.

Yes. Yes.

When it comes to handling pain, few things go down better than a big dose of laughter.

3. Laughter Massages Our Internal Organs

If you've ever treated yourself to a massage, you know what a delight it is to put your tired muscles and sore joints in the hands of a licensed massage therapist. Ahh.

Now, what about your kidneys? Don't they deserve a massage too? And your spleen. I'll bet you haven't thought about your poor spleen all day, but it's in there saying, "Me too! Me too!"

Laughter massages your inside muscles like a therapist massages your outside muscles. The late Norman Cousins called it *internal jogging*, an exercise for which your organs are most grateful.

You won't have to wrap yourself in a towel or break out in a sweat, either. Just laugh loud and often, with gusto. A smile makes a great umbrella, but for inner massage, you'll need more than a smile. You'll need a solid twenty-minute workout of guffaws and giggles, hoots and honks.

Fifteen big laughs each day is what the experts tell us is our minimum daily adult requirement for laughter. Since toddlers supposedly laugh fifteen times an hour, your prescription is clear: Get yourself a two year old. Oh, you don't have to keep it! Ask any young mother at church if she might loan you her toddler for an hour—trust me, she'll be elated with the plan. Then lock yourself in a room with the little cutie and laugh when they do. Voila! You'll have your allotment of laughter and so will that mom, thanks to this unique Mother's Hour Out program.

Brenda from Indiana gave herself an unintentional workout. She worked in the laboratory of a small rural hospital that required her to sit on a high stool. "I sat down in my chair and immediately realized it had been lowered. This threw me off balance and the chair tipped back, throwing me gracefully to the floor."

When the lab department finally got their laughter under control, Brenda told her coworker, "If I didn't know better, I'd think I hit my head."

"You did!" she told her. "Three times on the way down!"

Upon surveying the damage, not only did Brenda have three bumps on her head, she also had paint on her shirt from hitting the wall so hard. Brenda's intense form of internal and external massage proved one thing, she says: "Germans really are hardheaded."

4. Laughter Exercises Our Facial Muscles

Fifteen facial muscles get involved when we laugh, which is why after a good bout of laughter your cheeks hurt. That's their way of telling you, "Please do this more often, so it won't hurt so much." You know the dangers of being a weekend jogger. The same thing happens when we don't exercise those facial muscles often enough.

Laughter should make us feel wonderful all over. Andrea from Pennsylvania concurs. "It feels so good to laugh. Just like the good feeling after exercising but with less work." Donna from Virginia confesses laughing is "the only exercise my body gets," and Jackie from Colorado insists it's "impossible to live without it. Like oxygen, food, God."

Sustenance indeed.

Was life meant to be fun? Of course. Not every minute of every day, but often enough that it won't hurt when we chuckle. Of all the muscles we're given to work with, our laugh muscles should never be allowed to atrophy.

A merry heart does good, like medicine
But a broken spirit dries the bones.
(Proverbs 17:22)

The medical community and the spiritual community are (amazingly!) in agreement about the value of laughter. Doctors are known to keep lists of strange words and phrases patients use to describe their ills, for later peer review and aerobic laughing. Patients have complained of migrating headaches, prospect glands, abstract teeth, and hideous hernias. One patient wanted a scat can of his brain, and another sought a better remedy than what he'd been using for muscle pain: Soybean, Jr.

We'd better exercise whatever muscles we have left, because as we age they take on a mind of their own. Linda laughs when she remembers the days of her youth "when we had to have the same garment in different colors. Now, in my menopausal mid-forties, I have to have the same color outfit in two different *sizes*. Hmm. Which one can I get into this week?!"

Gravity and atrophy start much sooner than that, as Cheryl's thirtysomething body has convinced her.

"The other day I was standing half-dressed at the bathroom mirror while my five-year-old daughter watched intently."

"Mommy," she asked, "why is the skin on your tummy all wrinkly like that?"

Cheryl explained, "My tummy had to stretch a lot when I was carrying you and your brothers before you were born, so the skin never quite went all the way back."

Her daughter pondered that explanation for a moment. "Kinda like a balloon that's lost its air, huh?"

"Uh, yes, dear, kind of like that."

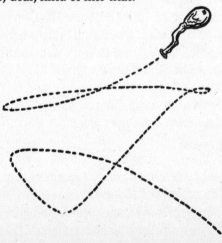

"But, Mommy," she continued, pointing to Cheryl's legs, "Why are your knees all wrinkly?"

Cheryl looked down at her knees. By golly, they were getting wrinkly! Now she was starting to get a bit discouraged.

"Well, honey, that's what happens to your skin when you get a little older," Cheryl replied.

Her daughter eyed her up and down for a few moments more, her blue eyes widening. "Will your whole body get like that? I guess your skin just gets tired and gives up, huh?"

Yes, darlin', that's pretty much how it works. But I'm convinced if we can keep our laugh muscles limber and the skin around our smiles moving, we're going to look gorgeous all the way to glory!

5. Laughter Improves Circulation

It's a common phenomenon I've seen time and again when I'm performing in a chilly room. The women are all folded in on themselves, like beautiful roses freshly delivered from the florist and still cool to the touch—arms folded, legs crossed, a sweater or jacket pulled around their shoulders.

Then they start laughing. Their jacket slips off. Their arms unfold so they can slap the table. Their legs uncross so they can bend over with laughter. Soon their faces are flushed with a warm glow, their fingers and toes are no longer stiff with cold, and they've literally blossomed, just like roses.

Since laughter increases the heart rate, it's only natural that it would increase blood flow and therefore circulation. What a health benefit, especially for those who are cold-blooded! Such was not the case for Charla from Georgia. She and her friend are both minister's wives. "Our husbands always joke that they need to go through and bless the house after we've been together laughing because we get so out of control."

One day they were both laughing so hard that "my friend raised her hand to wipe her eyes, and I doubled over at the same time. We met in the middle. Her thumb jabbed my eye so hard I almost cried—it was scratched and red and hurt for days—but at the time it made us laugh even harder."

When people asked about her bruised red-and-black eye, Charla just laughed. Her friend told people that "if she gets on my nerves again, I'll poke the other eye."

6. Laughter Oxygenates the Body

You were hoping I'd tell you that laughter was aerobic, yes? It's true. You can exhale up to seventy-five miles an hour with a big laugh. Gale warning! It would be prudent not to sit in front of someone with false teeth.

It's pure physiology: To laugh out, you must breathe in. Air is involved, so it has aerobic potential. Whether one could do sustained laughter for twenty minutes at your target heart rate, three times a week is anyone's guess. But think how delightful it would be to try.

Wendy from Colorado was simply trying to find out what the problem was with the air in their apartment. "My husband and I hadn't been feeling well for a week, so I called the gas company to see if there could be a gas leak. They transferred me to 911, and in less than five minutes, we heard sirens near our apartment. The doorbell rang, and five paramedics rushed in to see if we were okay. My husband said, 'What have you done this time?!'"

The paramedics took their blood pressures and checked out their apartment. Everything was fine, except for trying to explain it all to the neighbors who were staring at them through the windows, barely breathing.

7. Laughter Stimulates the Immune System

As a member of the American Association for Therapeutic Humor *and* the Fellowship of Merry Christians, I love discovering the many exciting ways that the Lord has fashioned our bodies to renew themselves. In a spiritual sense, you are to be "transformed by the renewing of your mind, that you may prove what is that good and acceptable and perfect will of God" (Romans 12:2).

Your body renews itself with all the basic necessities—food, oxygen, water, sleep, shelter from the elements, air. But there are many less tangible things that help us stay or get well—hugs, companionship, music, compassion, and, yes, laughter. When our bodies are being cared for properly, we produce T cells, the good blood cells that fight infection.

Laughter is one of the things that produce T cells. I don't have to understand it scientifically to rejoice in the reality that tee-hees make *T*s!

Sharon from Ohio and her husband joined another couple at a convention in Hawaii. "We spent a wonderful week sightseeing and touring the islands. We were amazed by all the open-air architecture. Many places featured lobbies with tropical birds, beautiful ponds with large fish, and intricate fountains made from lava.

"On our last night in Honolulu, we were proceeding through such a lobby, headed for dinner, when we got separated by a large group. My husband turned back to look for us, and suddenly could not feel solid ground beneath his rear foot. He began to teeter and sway, back and forth, struggling to maintain his balance.

"As I moved toward him, I watched him lose the balance battle and tumble backward, right into a rock fountain! He managed to land in a sitting position between the underwater fountain jets and lighting, with only his head unsubmerged

As he was helped out of the fountain, he nearly pulled his rescuers in with him!

"Other than a few scrapes from the rock, he was uninjured—except for his pride. We couldn't look at him without breaking into laughter. Typical of his good nature, he decided he'd provided a good story for everyone to take home with them from Hawaii."

A fresh floral lei will wither, and photos are stuck in a drawer, but that T cell–producing story will live on and on and on.

CHAPTER 21

Humor and Healing: It Only Hurts When I (Don't) Laugh

There's lots of people in this world who spend so much time watching their health that they haven't the time to enjoy it.
—Josh Billings

When I spoke in Louisiana a few years ago, the *Times-Picayune* published a feature article about my visit, with a big headline—LAUGHTER IS GOOD FOR YOUR BODY—and a photo of my abundant body underneath it. People must have opened their papers and said, "Wow! Miracle-Gro!" It's one thing to suggest that humor is good for you in the physical sense. Plenty of research has confirmed that truth, and there are whole books on the subject of the physiological benefits of laughing out loud.

Yes, humor helps, but can it heal? Is it that effective a prescription? Many of us think so. Betty from Oklahoma shares, "Humor has brought me back physically, emotionally, and spiritually. It kept me from going over the edge in a very low, depressed period of my life. Being able to laugh through the tears is a healing process."

Nurses often use humor to gauge a recovering patient's progress. They'll throw out a gentle joke and see how the patient responds. Even a smile indicates they're on the path toward wellness. Wise is the patient who knows humor's ability to assist the healing process and who looks for it at every turn.

Bowed Over

Catherine from New Jersey has a five-year-old granddaughter named Valerie who loves to wear pretty barrettes and bows in her hair. Looking through an old box of odds and ends, Valerie found a huge, pink Minnie Mouse bow with white polka dots.

"Mom, can I wear this to school tomorrow?" she asked.

Her mother cautioned, "It might be better just to wear it at home, Valerie, so the other children won't make fun of you."

But Valerie was determined to wear that bow. The next day after school, her mother met her at the bus stop, and there was that big pink bow on her head, along with a very happy smile.

"My teacher told me she hoped I'd wear it again because every time she looked at me, it made her smile!" Valerie announced.

Young Valerie learned something about humor and healing that day. Her teacher had been going through chemotherapy treatments for cancer, and as Valerie's grandmother sees it, "That big, pink, polka-dotted bow was the best medicine of all."

Judy from Texas fought—and won—a battle with breast cancer. "The Lord and laughter were what helped me to remain strong. After radiation, I developed asthma and couldn't laugh without coughing and losing my breath. I demanded that the doctors fix it! Not being able to laugh was the biggest disaster of my life."

Surviving and Thriving

The first time I spoke to a cancer survivor group on the healing power of humor, I feared that (1) they might argue with me, and (2) they might not have the ability to laugh. Wrong on both counts. They laughed with utter abandon and embraced what many of them already knew to be true: Humor helps us heal.

Beulah's own battle with breast cancer also ended in victory—and a mastectomy. "Since my bra size is 44 DD, it was necessary to get a prosthesis. On Labor Day I was at a family camp where they have a 360-degree water slide into the lake. I didn't have a bathing suit and decided to chance it in street clothes. After my second trip down, I started out of the water and discovered something was missing.

A woman nearby asked her, "What are you looking for?"

"My breast form!" Beulah gasped.

"Does it float?"

"I don't know, I've never lost it before!"

Twenty yards out into the lake they spotted it, floating among the lily pads. The woman offered to swim out and get it for her. Beulah says, "She brought 'Sally' back to me, I put her where she belonged, laughed a lot, hugged the woman, and went back up the hill to slide again and again, each time making sure everything was where it belonged!"

A Laugh or Death Situation

Humor and cancer may seem like odd bedfellows, but in truth, every survivor I've ever talked to confirms the benefits of maintaining, even enhancing, one's sense of humor through the recovery process. Karleen from Indiana shares, "My daughter had just undergone surgery for ovarian cancer for the second time, and upon returning to her room, she found several of us waiting for her, including her husband, Robert."

"Oh, Robert," her daughter said, "don't look so sad. I'm going to be all right. God put me in your life to make you miserable, and I'm not through yet!"

What an incredible testimony to this woman's faith, strength, and ability to overcome adversity with humor. As Golda Meir said, "Those who do not know how to weep with their whole heart, don't know how to laugh either."

Phyllis from Michigan says, "I truly believe laughter is God's pain medicine for the hurts of life. No matter what valley we go through, God provides a way to rejoice in him always, and sometimes that's through laughter."

Lori from Texas is a valley-overcomer as well. When her husband was diagnosed with pancreatic cancer that had spread to his lungs, she was devastated. "My two best friends immediately came to the rescue. Yes, there was some crying, but there was a lot of laughing. They told me everything funny they could think of and made up some stuff.

"My husband is really not a laugher, but since his diagnosis, we've watched funny movies and laughed. We make it a fun day when we have to go to get chemotherapy, and I look for funny things to tell the other patients to get them laughing too."

Marilyn declares, "Humor has seen me through two heart-valve operations and long stays in the hospital. I'm living a life that I was told I had only a 5 percent chance of having. Through all of that, I've learned to laugh at life. If I'm going to be here only a short while, I sure better learn to enjoy it."

What an encouragement when we read the words of our Lord, "Blessed are you who weep now, / For you shall laugh" (Luke 6:21). We do find humor in some of the most unexpected, somber situations.

Kelly from Colorado writes of a friend of the family who lost a loved one. "The brother of the deceased had placed his new, never-before-worn suit in one of the bedroom closets. It came time to dress for the funeral, but the new suit was nowhere to be found.

"When the brother viewed the deceased, guess what the man in the coffin was wearing?! Apparently when they needed clothes for the body, they assumed that everything in the closet belonged to the deceased!"

Death is never funny. But it can be joyous. If a person is set free from pain and suffering, knowing that their Savior waits at the gates of heaven to welcome them home, those of us attending the funeral can smile at one another without apology.

Laughter is exactly what filled the air at Lucille's funeral. Shirley from Indiana loved her "adopted" grandmother Lucille, who was over ninety and nearly blind. As she talked to her on the phone one morning, she heard a man's voice in the background.

"Oh, if you have company, you can call me later," Shirley suggested.

Lucille laughed. "No, no that's just Sam. He was here late last night, so I had him spend the night."

"You did what?!?"

Through her chuckles, Lucille explained, "Sam is my new talking clock." Sam-the-clock was her constant companion in and out of the hospital. She carried Sam at her elbow at all times. Upon her death the family decided to put Sam in the casket nestled in Lucille's arms as he had been for the last several weeks of her life.

At her funeral service, the pastor had just said, "Let us pray," when Sam spoke in his deep, husky voice, "It is now 11:00 A.M."

Shirley confesses, "The room was filled with uncontrollable laughter instead of grief, exactly as Lucille would have wanted it."

There Is a Balm in Gilead

Mary from Michigan took her ninetysomething mother into the hospital for a minor ailment.

"I'm thinking about changing doctors," the elderly woman announced.

"Why, Mother?" a surprised Mary asked.

"I've doctored with this man for forty years, and I'm not a bit better!"

The Lord designed humor not only for our physical well-being, but for our emotional and spiritual health as well. That's exactly how Mary from Kansas sees it. "I believe laughter is a healing gift, for the emotions and the spirit. It feels like a cleansing internal bath to rinse out pain, anger, and self-pity."

Bobbie from South Australia agrees, "Humour has saved my life. Being able to look for a laugh at the everyday quirky, bizarre, and madcap events going on around me—and which I have sometimes created—has provided a healing balm as I've battled grief and mental illness and worked through to healing and peace. And I'm still laughing!"

Donna had 'em laughing in Virginia as the coordinator at her agency for a program that promotes healthy attitudes, exercise, and so forth. "The quarterly regional meeting was being held at a state-operated psychiatric/mental-health facility. Attendees were asked to dress as though we were going to a Hawaiian luau. Out of the fifty people there, I was the only one in costume. You can imagine the looks I received, strolling the halls of a mental-health facility in a grass skirt!"

Cheri from Florida thinks laughter has not only therapeutic value but cosmetic value as well. "I look much better in smiles than frowns." And Sherry from Washington concludes, "There is no life without humor. My very well-being is dependent on humor."

Humor is by no means the only positive emotional experience that promotes healing. Love and affection make all the difference in the world—the love of God and the love of people you care about. Faith and hope walk beside love and laughter, as do the patients' will to live and the unique calling that gives their lives meaning. There is great comfort to be found in glorious music, delicious scents, the beauty of nature, and the warmth of light.

And yes, laughter weaves its carefree way through all those joy-filled, purpose-filled, spirit-filled needs. We humans are a complex bunch. Only the One who knows us and loves us completely has the power to meet every one of those needs in so personal a way that we feel he is ministering to us alone.

The one who knows God can laugh in the face of death because to die with Christ in your heart is to live—and laugh—with him, forever.

As Brenda Sees It

I received a very moving letter from Brenda in Florida. She works with cancer patients, particularly with women who have breast cancer. As a physician assistant in oncology, she explains, "All my patients have refractory cancer of some sort (primarily breast cancer, leukemia, lymphoma, myeloma) which has failed all therapies. Their final chance at a cure is with high-dose intensive chemotherapy followed by bone marrow transplant rescue.

"A high number of patients do not survive the therapy and, unfortunately, a large number relapse after this difficult and prolonged treatment."

Already you are probably shaking your head, as I did, wondering how this woman can go to work every day and face this grim reality.

Brenda wrote, "I love working with these patients and their families, and I really feel this is a ministry for me. I think that the Lord has given me the gift of encouragement. I know that for many people this would be a difficult area to serve, but I really love my work. These patients teach me so much. I definitely am learning which things should be priorities in life—my spiritual life, my family life, and my relationships—and what kind of things are not worth worrying about."

Not everyone who laughs in the face of death overcomes it in the physical sense. Yet humor has a place even in the dying process. Ask Brenda. Ask a hospice volunteer. Ask those who loved comedian Gilda Radner, who died in 1989 suffering from ovarian cancer, which she called "the most un-funny thing in the world."

Brave Gilda told Bob, her radiation technician, that he was the funniest person she'd ever met. (This from a woman married to Gene Wilder!) People always told Bob that he should be on television, but Gilda disagreed. "No, he should be in the radiation therapy department, because that is where his humor is needed most."

You will be sorrowful, but your sorrow will be turned into joy. (John 16:20)

When Laughter and Forgiveness Seem Long Ago and Far Away

Maritza came to hear me speak in Florida recently, and when she responded to our survey for this book, she gave me some crucial insights that I asked her to share with you as well.

There's nothing humorous about this story at all, but it is, in its own way, joy filled.

There are tragic moments that challenge us to the core of our being. Faith and forgiveness appear beyond our grasp, let alone joy and laughter. We doubt, in fact, that we will ever laugh again.

Our only hope and comfort then—as always—is found in the promises of God:

Weeping may endure for a night,
But joy comes in the morning. (Psalm 30:5)

Maritza explains, "One June, while my husband was pastoring a small church in Illinois, our church hosted a Vacation Bible School kickoff picnic at a local park. A woman from the church accidentally drove a malfunctioning van through the pavilion where we were gathered, striking and killing our seventeen-month-old son, Nathan, who was sleeping in his stroller.

"The years that have followed have been extremely painful and difficult. Although always an upbeat and a funny person myself, these years have been filled with many tears and hours of desperation and loss. I hesitated to attend your conference, Liz, afraid you would somehow hint that everything was a laughable situation, and I know all too well it is not."

[I would never do such a thing, of course, but you can easily understand her fears.]

She writes, "I'm so thankful I went, because certainly the laughter was good, and it was so easy to identify with all the examples you gave. You said that laughter doesn't make you forget or dismiss your sufferings, but helps you survive and get through it. Exactly! Thanks so much for a lovely day."

Bless you, Maritza, for sharing your journey with all of us who need that reminder. Suffering is neither fun, nor funny. We stand on his promises, weep with those who will weep with us, and wait for joy to return to our doorstep, as it most surely will.

Those who sow in tears
Shall reap in joy. (Psalm 126:5)

CHAPTER 22

Humor as a Stress-Reliever: Joy Comes in the Morning, Unless You Wake Up on the Wrong Side of the Bed

*With the fearful strain that is on me night and day,
if I did not laugh I should die.*
—Abraham Lincoln

"One morning, my young son woke up in a terrible mood," writes Sue from Kentucky. "I told him he'd gotten up on the wrong side of the bed."

"But, Mom!" he protested. "The other side is against the wall!"

Offspring Angst

Children and stress—a package deal. Better keep your sense of humor handy. Those of us with younger kids have one sort of stress; those with teenagers smile through gritted teeth and say, "Just you wait!"

Day-to-day stress isn't as dramatic as the stress of facing catastrophic illness or death, but drip by drip, even the daily load of stress we carry can add up.

"It never fails," Sheryl from Oklahoma sighs. "Whenever I go into my boys' rooms to tuck them in for the night, I end up fuming. Clothes here and there, socks on the ceiling fan, toys in the dirty clothes hampers, Big Macs under the mattress, last month's chocolate milk in a glass hidden behind Mr. Bear on the headboard."

We get the picture.

She tells them, "Boys, I hate to come up here and find this mess all the time! Why is it so hard to keep your rooms picked up?"

Her middle child of three boys calmly looked up at her one evening after one of her tirades about the messy rooms and simply said, "Well, Mom, just don't come up here then."

Sheryl laughs. "The simple solutions of a child! I laughed and laughed. God eased my distressed conditon even if just for a few moments at the end of my hectic day."

Ellen from Pennsylvania, also the mother of three boys, had a particularly rough and tiring day. "I went upstairs to rest while my husband fixed supper. Thirty minutes later, my three sons—ages eight, six, and three—trooped into my bedroom.

"Usually a rambunctious crew, they stood quietly by the door, eyeing me cautiously. Trying to muster some energy, I exclaimed, 'Well, isn't this nice! Did you come to get me for supper?'"

They looked at one another, then the oldest ventured, "Nah. Dad said you were stressed out, and we just wanted to see what that looked like."

Choose Joy, Question Boy

When stress arrives at your doorstep (actually, it may live there, but let's not dwell on that), you have a choice in how you respond to it:

1. Scream with anger
2. Cry with anguish
3. Laugh with abandon

The best choice is so obvious. There is a time and place for righteous anger, and tears are wonderfully cleansing too. But in the face of daily stress, Option 3 wins by a country (s)mile.

Linda from Oklahoma stumbled on a great stress-relieving way to handle the horrors of having a dating daughter. She sent me *An Application to Date Our Daughter*. Requests on the detailed, one-page form included a demand for "a complete financial statement, history, lineage, and current medical report from your doctor."

What else did they need to know about prospective dates for their daughter? Here's the hilarious list:

Do you own—
 A van?
 A truck with oversize tires?
 A water bed?
 An earring, nose ring, or belly-button ring?
 A tattoo?
 (If yes to any of the above, discontinue application and leave premises immediately.)

Their "application" also required short essays on:

What does *late* mean to you?
What does *abstinence* mean to you?
The one thing I hope this application does not ask me about
is . . .

It concluded with:

Please allow four to five years for processing.

Maybe Susan from Pennsylvania should have created a similar questionnaire for her eight-year-old son who brings wildlife of another sort home, "all types of wildlife, tame or otherwise," she explains. "He'd recently bought a snake from a pet store, a very snakey-looking snake.

"I use my feet to propel my wheelchair. One day as I was wheeling down the hardwood floors in the hall, our son said, 'Mom, stop with the noise. You're scaring my snake.'"

Wait . . .who is scaring whom here?!

Fowl Play

Sometimes parents experience humor by watching their children mature. Lucille from New Mexico finds fun in how her parents are maturing. "After they retired, my mother and father lived out on the California desert with a little orchard, a small vegetable garden, and a pen full of guinea fowl. Though guinea eggs are smaller than chicken eggs, my parents claimed guineas had much more personality than chickens."

I didn't know chickens had any personality at all, did you? And do eggs from high-personality guineas—Sunnies, no doubt—taste better than those from, say, Foggy fowls?

Lucille continues, "Often the guinea hens expressed their personality through a raucous squawk. My mother was convinced the guineas understood words. And sometimes they gave that impression. They had two favorite calls that they frequently screeched. Every time anyone went out the back door, one guinea or another would begin to squawk something that sounded like, 'Stupid! Stupid! Stupid!' or 'Go back! Go back! Go back!'

"One day my mother washed a sheet and took it out the back door to hang on the clothesline. A guinea started a warning squawk, 'Go back! Go back! Go back!' A stiff breeze was blowing from the Pacific Ocean. When my mother opened up the sheet to toss it over the line, a gust of wind suddenly grabbed the sheet, slapped it against her face, and wrapped it all around her.

"While she was struggling to get out of the wet sheet, she heard a raucous squawk, 'Stupid! Stupid! Stupid!'"

It is not clear who is the most stressed out here: (*a*) the daughter with the guinea-loving parent, or (*b*) the sheet-draped mother, or (*c*) the bright mind trapped in the body of a guinea hen.

Kodiak Moments
(In Other Words, a Bear)

Laughter as a means of stress release is hardly a new discovery. In 1860 Herbert Spencer called laughter a "safety valve" for excess energy in the nervous system. For me, the first sign of stress is losing my sense of humor, and the first sign of relief is a loud guffaw.

Carol from Kentucky is the kind of woman who spares herself the stress and sees the humor in the moment ASAP. The second-floor bathroom pipe broke, on her birthday, no less, and her house was flooded all the way to the basement. "Floors buckled, two ceilings caved in, the heat went off, and for a while I didn't have running water. My friends had given me a surprise party the weekend before, so when the construction crew (wrecking crew?) arrived, all the decorations were still hanging from the remaining ceilings and walls. The crew was very polite and wished me a Happy Birthday!"

And, we can only hope, offered a birthday discount.

You never know what stress will make you say or do. Arlene from Michigan was in a car accident. While riding in the ambulance, the attendants asked her some simple questions to see if she was okay.

"How old are you?" the EMT asked.

"I don't know," Arlene admitted.

"How much do you weigh?"

"A hundred and thirty pounds."

"You weigh less than that."

"Good."

"Who is the president of the United States?"

"Mrs. Clinton."

Sometimes medical personnel giggle under their masks at a stressed-out patient, but it does work the other way around as well. Barbara from Georgia worked as a nurse in a busy intensive care unit. "One day things were particularly chaotic and busy. The nurses were running around tending to numerous crises that were all occurring at the same time, doctors were shouting out orders, the phone was ringing off the hook, patients were calling for help, meal trays were arriving, family members were trying to get the nurse's attention to ask questions . . . it was a madhouse.

"One nurse in our unit tended to be a little scatterbrained to begin with. She was running to and fro when she stopped to answer the buzzing intercom. With exhaustion and exasperation in her voice, she pushed the intercom button and said to the entire family-waiting-room area, 'Can you help me?'"

She quickly corrected herself and said, "I mean, can I help you?"

The staff could hear laughter coming back over the intercom from the waiting room as a man's voice responded, "I think you were right the first time."

A Real Flag-Waver

"Unexpected humor has a way of making me feel more positive and healthier," suggests Barbara from Texas. "It is a wonderful stress buster and helps me keep my life in perspective."

Forgive me for one more funereal example of unexpected humor, but Gloria from Washington offers a story we can all identify with. "At my father's funeral, God bless his soul, my siblings and I gathered with fifty other mourners at the graveside. As the bugle blew taps, four young military men solemnly folded the American flag."

Or tried to.

"These men could not fold the flag right! The stars of the flag were folding under, not on top. On the third attempt, my family and I broke out into uncontrolled laughter. However, the people behind us thought that we had broken out into uncontrolled sobbing (because in an attempt to control our laughing, we had covered our faces).

"Meanwhile, the poor young military men did not even crack a smile, which made us laugh even harder. The fourth attempt was their last. I have not seen four young men disappear from a scene so fast."

My own two sisters and I made it through my mother's funeral without laughing, but not without crying. What a sad, sad day, more than twenty years ago. But that evening back at the house, the three of us were sitting around talking about what Mom would have thought of the service and got tickled. I have no idea now what it was that set us off, but that's not the point. The point is, three adult women went from crying to laughing in a matter of seconds. I don't think the tears even shifted gears, they just kept flowing.

When you laugh until you cry, or cry until you laugh, the effect is pretty much the same—red face, scrunched up expression, drippy mascara, wet cheeks, wrung-out tissue, stress gone.

Humor As Oops-Catcher

Jeanette from Ohio has a daughter who sounds much like our sweet Lillian, which is to say, "quite dramatic. Everything requires Scarlett O'Hara-type acting. One day when she was told that she couldn't play until her homework was done," Jeanette says, "she wilted to the floor, moaning and covering her face.

"When it was obvious we weren't budging, she crawled up the stairs and flung herself facedown on the bed. Moaning and crying was all we could hear, which made her father and me start laughing. When we looked in on her, she seemed to be struggling to keep up the act.

"I repeated my directions to finish her homework and added, 'No matter what you do, don't laugh! Don't do it!' She got quiet and wiggled. We kept saying, 'Don't laugh!' and of course she couldn't keep a straight face. Soon, we were all laughing."

Many parents use this time-honored technique (we sure do), and it truly does work, for all the parties involved.

Bonnie's son worked in the produce section of a grocery store where he was approached by a woman asking for half a head of lettuce. "My son said he almost went bonkers and dashed back behind those flip-floppy doors to consult with his manager."

He told his manager rather loudly that there was a "first-class nut" out there who wanted half a head of lettuce. As he and his manager walked back out into the store, there stood the little lady, who'd obviously heard the whole conversation.

Bonnie's brilliant son bent down, put his arm around the lady's shoulder and said to his manager, "And this is the sweet, precious lady who wants the other half!"

CHAPTER 23

❦

Humor and Perspective: Someday We'll Laugh About This

It would be argument for a week, laughter for a month, and a good jest forever.
—William Shakespeare

We've all been in high-stress, low-strength situations where we turn to the next person and sigh, "Someday we'll laugh about this."

I say, why wait? If you can see the humor potential, dive right in. The time and distance between the dastardly deed and your ability to laugh at it is what I call the *stress zone*. You can't hurry the time, but you can decrease the distance, emotionally and mentally, between the first and last moment you spend in the stress zone.

You have to stand back, literally sometimes, to see the Big Picture, to put the thing in perspective, to chop the problem back down to size. It's a universal need, this perspective business. Melinda from Texas thinks "humor lets us see ourselves and others in a different light." A more flattering light, I'd say. "It makes me relax and realize that most crises are not really that important," says Betty from Missouri. Marguerette from Maine wisely points out that laughter "makes bad times and good times both better," and Barbara from Kentucky offers the ultimate challenge: "Why take life so seriously? You're never going to get out of it alive anyway."

Well, there's always that.

Our favorite funny fella, Bill Cosby, said, "If you can find humor in anything, you can survive it."

Someday We'll Laugh About This

The following ten true stories are exactly the kind of situations that must have produced that someday-we'll-laugh-about-this response at the moment of impact. Obviously, the principal players did laugh about it eventually, or they'd never have sent their tale to me for a book about humor!

Take 1

LaRee from Washington was visiting southern California and decided to drop in to surprise her aunt and cousin. "We arrived unannounced. The front door was open, so I quietly walked in. A man was asleep on the couch with a pillow over his head. Certain it was my cousin, I jerked the pillow off his head and said, 'All right, get up!'"

Boy, was he surprised. LaRee too. Her aunt and cousin had moved.

Take 2

New neighbors had moved next door to Bonnie from Michigan. "They moved in around March and, sad to say, it was June and I still hadn't introduced myself.

"The first nice weekend of the summer, I went out to work my flower beds, wearing a perfectly good pair of shorts I'd discovered in my giveaway pile, not at all sure how they ended up in there.

"My new neighbors pulled up, and I decided to greet them and make up for lost time. I was my most friendly outgoing self, but they appeared a little standoffish."

Later, she shared her assessment of the new neighbors with her husband, who offered an observation: "Honey, maybe they acted odd because the zipper in your white shorts is completely undone."

Maybe so.

Bonnie confesses, "It's been hard for me to look them in the eyes ever since!"

Take 3

"My mother bought my father a birthday cake," shares Kim from Alabama, "and she invited some relatives over to celebrate, hiding the cake in her bedroom to keep it as a surprise. Later, being the helpful daughter I was, I took it upon myself to bring the cake out.

"Just as they realized I was missing, I came out of the bedroom, tripped, and dumped the cake upside-down on the floor. Lucky for me the cake was in a box. Mom picked it up, scraped the frosting off the inside of the lid, and kept going like nothing happened."

Go, Mom.

Take 4

Dinner was at a Chinese restaurant for Marilyn from Michigan and her family, including Sheryl, her twelve-year-old daughter. "Sheryl ordered the *human* pork, and our dignified Oriental waiter very politely told her she must mean the *Hunan* pork. Her brothers were less polite and didn't let her forget it all through her teen years.

"Then Sheryl had the privilege of spending a summer teaching in China. She waited eagerly for her assignment, hoping it might be in one of the northern provinces so she could see the Great Wall. Instead, it was in one of the southern provinces.

"God does have a sense of humor!" Sheryl declared. Her assignment? Hunan!

Take 5

Jo from California had every mother's worst nightmare come true. "My three-year-old son was playing in the yard while I got ready to go shopping. When I went outside, there was no sign of him.

"I calmly told myself that he'd probably gone to visit one of our neighbors, but after making the rounds and finding that no one had seen him, I began to panic. There were numerous construction sites on our block that posed many dangers. Even worse, someone could have taken my son.

"I got in my car and began looking for him, asking every person I met if they had seen a little boy with a red shirt on. Several times I got the same answer, 'Yes, he was headed that direction. He said he was trying to find his dog.'

"If I didn't find him soon I realized I would have to call the police to report my child missing. By now I was nearly hysterical. I continued to drive up and down various streets, but my eyes were so blurred by tears that I could hardly see.

"Finally, as a last resort, I stopped my car in the middle of the street and screamed my son's name. A small voice answered, 'I'm right here, Mommy.'

"As my eyes came back into focus, I couldn't believe what I was seeing. There sat my son on some stranger's lawn, happily playing with a toy their youngster had left out in their front yard."

Apparently it never occurred to her son that he was lost.

"I ran to him and scooped him up into my arms, not wanting to ever let him go. Between sobs and kisses, I told him how much I loved him, how worried I had been that something horrible had happened to him, and how happy I was that he was safe.

"Still shaking, I drove home and told him repeatedly never ever to leave our yard without a grown-up again. Even after we got home, I was so shook up that I could not stop crying.

"After about twenty minutes of this, my son looked at me and said matter-of-factly, 'Mom, if you can't stop crying, just go to your room.'"

Take 6

Shari's father-in-law was a minister at two country churches in southern Indiana. He'd had many medical complications in his life, but he also had a wonderful sense of humor. He was fully sighted in one eye and had a glass eye in the other.

Traveling through a busy intersection, his car was hit in the rear end by another driver. Both men got out to assess the damage.

Shari says, "The other driver was a wreck. He was an emotional basket case and started to carry on about his bad heart. My father-in-law said very calmly to him, 'Well, buddy, I don't know what you're complaining about. I'm blind.'"

Take 7

It was the kind of summer that memories are made of. Karla from Washington was twelve when her family spent a long summer vacation roaming around the countryside in a camper.

They'd just spent the night in the Canadian Rockies, and Karla awakened to find that her mother and father "had outdone themselves preparing breakfast. The outdoor picnic table at the campsite was loaded with all kinds of good-looking, wonderful-smelling goodies.

"My sister and I helped set the table, and everything was ready. The rest of the family were still getting dressed, so I sat down on one side of the picnic table (the kind with benches attached), and my mother sat down right beside me on the same bench.

"In all this time, no one had noticed that the table was situated on a slope, and my mother had just added herself to the downhill side of the equation. The next thing either of us knew, we were sprawled on our backs with our feet up in the air and wearing the entire breakfast!

"Both my mother and I were stunned for an instant until we looked at each other and a low rumble of laughter began building. You gain new respect for your mother when you see her with gooey banana-bread frosting on her face! And I admit, I looked quite special with a bowl of peach slices in my hair.

"We laughed for at least ten minutes before we even attempted to get up from the mess, and our entire family joined in. We've repaid the cost of the lost food thousands of times over in the laughter we still share over that one instant in time.

"We also check to make sure the picnic table is on level ground."

Take 8

"The Bicentennial Class of 1976 silently awaited their diplomas. The dignitaries sat in the front row—the principal, vice principal, coaches, and so on."

Garlene from Montana continues, "I was sitting a few rows behind these powerful people, and our row was called to accept our diplomas. I concentrated on not stepping on someone's robe or messing up the procession.

"Then it happened. I tripped into the person handing out the diplomas and knocked over the podium, the flowers, and the microphone. It all happened so fast that all I could do was laugh and turn beet red.

"The audience roared with laughter. Evidently I wasn't the only one experiencing anxiety that day. There was laughter everywhere except that first row.

It was, however, the main topic of conversation at Garlene's twentieth high-school reunion.

Take 9

Mary from Manitoba was coming home late from a meeting in town. "I noticed a car following me as soon as I turned off the highway onto a country road. Since my cousin had been held up under similar conditions I got scared.

"I slowed down to let the car pass, but it kept on following me. I imagined they would follow until we got a little farther from the highway and then attack.

"I panicked and decided to turn in to the first farmyard I came to and pretend I lived there. No use—they kept following! All was dark in the house, so what could I do but turn around?

As I did so, I came face-to-face with the people following me—the couple who lived there!"

Take 10

Kim from Louisiana learned a hard but funny lesson on her very first job as a registered nurse. "I'd had my three-day paperwork orientation and was now set to start on the ward. The hospital had given me a red ribbon to tape to my name tag to indicate, 'Hey, don't count on me for anything, I'm new.'

"The charge nurse's first words to me were, 'That red ribbon doesn't mean anything, you're taking a patient.'"

Gulp.

She gave Kim an elderly lady in her nineties who needed total care. The woman wasn't doing well, but the family wanted full measures taken to resuscitate her if she should stop breathing. "I must have looked really scared because Myrene, the LPN on duty, leaned over and said, 'It'll be okay.'

"About this time the maintenance man stuck his head in and announced that the call-light system was being repaired and couldn't be used. I was really starting to get upset because that system was the way to indicate an emergency when a nurse needed help. I asked Myrene, 'What should I do if I have problems?'"

Myrene answered, "Throw a bedpan in the hallway."

So off Kim went with her big metal bedpan to take care of her patient. "I thought I'd start with something safe and began to give her a bed bath. I finished the front. So far, so good. I turned her on her side to bathe her back, and she suddenly took one big breath, shuddered, and stopped breathing!

"I watched and watched and still no breath. With adrenaline pumping, fueled by fear, I threw the bedpan out the door."

Bad timing.

"The elderly woman's doctor was walking through the door just as I let go. The bedpan bounced off his temple, and he crumpled out cold in the doorway. The rest of the nurses had arrived with the code cart. They hauled the doctor into the hallway, left him there, and tried to resuscitate my patient.

"All I could do was stand in the corner and sob because I knew I had just lost my job!

"My patient, rest her soul, died. The doctor ended up in the hospital overnight with a hairline skull fracture and concussion. Meanwhile, as we were walking down the hallway, my mentor, Myrene, put her arm around my shoulder and said, 'I was just joking!'

"For months I couldn't carry a bedpan anywhere without people yelling, 'Incoming!'"

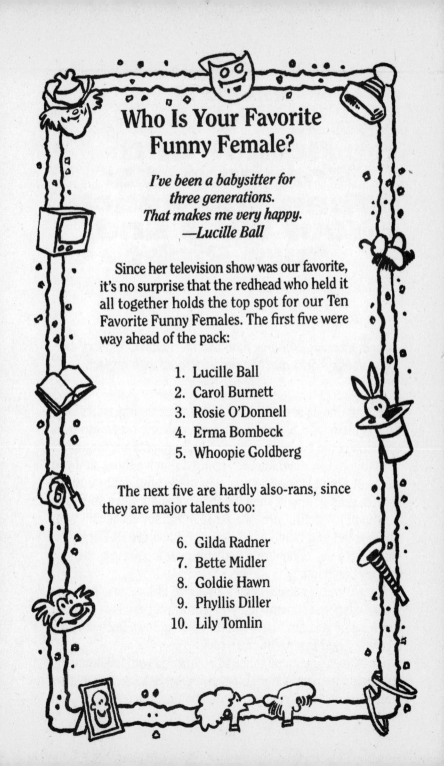

Who Is Your Favorite Funny Female?

*I've been a babysitter for
three generations.
That makes me very happy.*
—Lucille Ball

Since her television show was our favorite,
it's no surprise that the redhead who held it
all together holds the top spot for our Ten
Favorite Funny Females. The first five were
way ahead of the pack:

1. Lucille Ball
2. Carol Burnett
3. Rosie O'Donnell
4. Erma Bombeck
5. Whoopie Goldberg

The next five are hardly also-rans, since
they are major talents too:

6. Gilda Radner
7. Bette Midler
8. Goldie Hawn
9. Phyllis Diller
10. Lily Tomlin

CHAPTER 24

Humor and Forgiveness: When You Reach Your Wit's End, Turn Right

I am a great and sublime fool. But then I am God's fool and
all His works must be contemplated with respect.
—Mark Twain

When we do something foolish, embarrassing, ridiculous, or just plain silly, a certain amount of shame may wash over us. "How could I do such a thing?" we'll say, or "I am so stupid!"

Listen to Liz, now: Anybody could do such a thing, and you certainly aren't lacking wits . . . wit, maybe, but not brains! It's time to grab your wit, then laugh, pray, and forgive yourself.

One of my definitions of a sense of humor is the ability to understand and laugh at a joke—when you're it! Forgiving yourself is a way of honoring God's ultimate forgiveness extended in your direction.

Forgiveness is also a deep expression of love, and as Gayle from Oklahoma so aptly puts it, "You can't have love without humor, and you can't have humor without love. Both are gifts from God and cannot be revoked."

By all means, extend grace to others and yourself, knowing that being human is, well, normal. In fact, it's exactly what we were created to be, nothing more and nothing less.

The Handwriting Is on the Wall

"This is as funny as I get," wrote Dianne from Illinois. I'm not sure if that was an apology or a warning. She's a bookkeeper in a nursing home. "Some of our residents are not in tune with reality any longer (bless them). I was walking down the hall, and one of the cute little lady residents who usually lives in her own world asked me for an ink pen. I did not have one with me, so I made a special effort and hunted down a pen for her."

Uh-oh.

"I didn't think to ask her what she was planning to do with the ink pen. She'd sounded so normal, so with-it, that I just gave it to her without another thought.

"I found out later what she'd planned to do with it: She wrote part of a Scripture verse on our fresh, new wallpaper."

The bad news is, she wrote "Love is patient." The good news is, she didn't continue with the rest of 1 Corinthians 13!

"Let it be known that I have learned my lesson," says Dianne. "If anyone asks me for an ink pen, I ask what, where, when, who, why, and how is this pen going to be used before handing it over!"

Dianne wisely forgave the resident and herself. No word yet on her supervisor.

Cruisin'

Edie from Michigan was on a cruise with her husband. As she confesses, "I bought a special new outfit, sure to impress the others at our dinner table. I was convinced only the most influential people took cruises. Our first evening came, and I was seated next to a very distinguished-looking man who reminded me of Perry Como. We chatted through the first three courses until my curiosity wouldn't allow me to go on without inquiring about his occupation."

A Wall Street banker? Corporate CEO, perhaps?

"He was a farmer. I know the Lord had to be rolling with laughter. After my 'attitude check,' we had a wonderful voyage. One of the other 'farmers' at our table was a great tenor. He and I entered the talent contest later in the week and won first prize!"

Edie also gets first prize for humbly admitting her own mistaken impression, forgiving herself, and pressing on toward the fun.

How Old Did You Say You Were?

We've all had those down-in-the-dump days that refuse to go away. Sheila's mother-in-law was having one of those, and "decided to get her hair done and buy herself a new outfit."

After a productive visit to the salon and the mall, she stopped by the grocery on her way home. As Sheila describes it, "It was a beautiful summer day, and she was beginning to feel much better about herself. Her favorite bag boy helped her with the groceries as they carried on a bit of small talk."

She said to the nice young man, "I hear it's going to be eighty today."

He replied, "Oh, really? Well, happy birthday!"

Rumor has it she still shops at that grocery, but avoids small talk with the bag boys.

Rainy Day People

Ever had your ladies' retreat at a rustic campground in the pouring-down rain? I've attended a few, I've spoken at many, and that was the situation for Shirley, the keynote speaker on this particular rainy weekend.

She confesses, "As I sloshed through the rain, my spirit was as drenched as my hair. I whispered to God that I was not grateful for the situation he had put me in!

"After being introduced, I stood up to face my audience and realized none of them looked any better than I did. I told them so, we all laughed, and then we were ready to listen to what God had to say—especially me."

Once again, extending forgiveness to oneself is step one on the road to recovering your wit.

Hot Plates

My house is full of Fibber McGee closets. Crack the door open at your own risk, because who knows what might come tumbling out.

Paula from Wisconsin is my kind of woman. "One time when I was getting ready for a date with a new boyfriend, I didn't have time to do the dishes, so I just threw them in the oven temporarily.

"At the end of the date, we stopped at Shakey's for pizza. Since they were closing up for the night, we brought the pizza back to my place."

Where they could heat it up in her oven.

Her date was the one who flipped open the oven door and found the dishes. "I had to confess I wasn't the perfect housekeeper. He still asked me out after that anyway."

Most men would rather have a woman with a sense of humor than a clean house anyway, don't you think?

Tiger by the Tail

Cathy and Joe want to make sure you do not try this at home. We promise, we won't. Besides, it would require a big, fourteen-pound cat named Velcro for the starring role, and only Cathy and Joe have one of those.

"I had a helium-filled balloon out in the yard one day," Cathy begins. "Velcro, the curious cat, had to check out this balloon. For no reason I can explain, I loosely tied it to his tail. He didn't seem to mind since I would often tie a piece of yarn to his tail that he would chase for a long time.

"Joe and I were amused by this cat walking around the yard with his balloony tail up in the air when suddenly our terrier, Step, came around the corner and gave chase to the sporting Velcro, who made a fast run toward our nearby car.

"Before I could stop anything, Velcro dove under the car with his balloon in tow, which gave a very loud POP! Velcro flew out the other side and didn't stop running until he was way up in the woods. Joe and I were laughing so hard we were both lying down in the yard crying."

Cathy admits with great remorse, "Velcro was a little skittish for an hour or so after we got him to come back home, but otherwise he soon forgot the whole incident."

Forgive and forget—hey, if cats can do it, we humans should be able to manage to forgive ourselves, forget our follies, and find the humor that's hiding in our own backyard.

Merry-Go-Round Is Right!

Nancy was in her mid-twenties when she rode the merry-go-round at King's Island near Cincinnati. Lest you think she was a little old for that particular ride, I'll point out that her husband and mother-in-law had joined her.

"I hate heights," says Nancy, "and my horse was quite tall." Someone helped her up, but at the end of the ride she looked waaay down at the floor far beneath her and thought, *I guess you get off this thing like you would a real horse*.

She had her left foot in the stirrup and swung her right leg over the back of the horse. "Unfortunately, at this point the left stirrup flew up in the air with my foot stuck in it, and I landed under the horse's stomach with both legs wrapped in a death grip around the saddle and my hands hanging onto the pole!"

This is quite a picture.

To make matters worse, her horse was stationed at the entrance where people were winding in and out, so "there were probably three hundred people in total hysterics with a perfect view of all this.

"I yelled for my husband who hurried to my side, but he couldn't figure out what to grab hold of to get me off, and he was laughing so hard—along with the three hundred other people—that he was in a state of total relaxation. People were crying, tears rolling down their faces, many doubled over, and some laughing so hard that no noise came out at all, as I swung there, upside down, for a full five minutes.

"My greatest fear was that my horse would start back up with me still under it! Finally my left hand, from sheer exhaustion, slid down the pole, and I dropped off in a huge heap at the bottom. Every drop of blood in my body was in my face, both from hanging upside down and from sheer embarrassment.

"I thought, *Okay, well these people will never see me again anyway*. Boy was I wrong! Everywhere I went for the rest of the day somebody from the group of three hundred would recognize me and double over laughing when I came to a new ride."

I was there . . . weren't you?

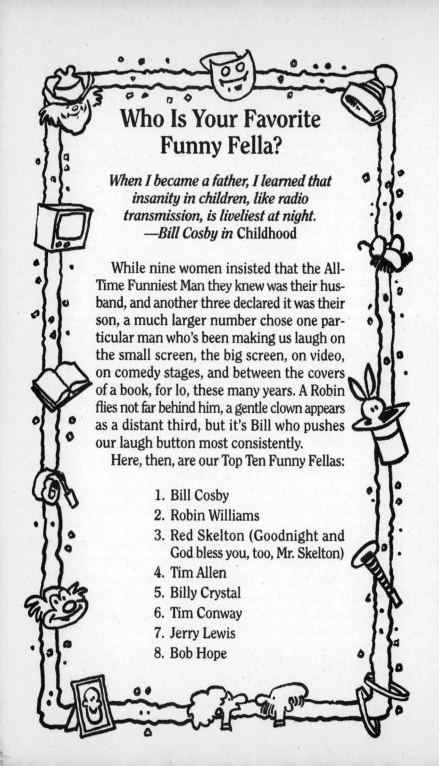

Who Is Your Favorite Funny Fella?

When I became a father, I learned that insanity in children, like radio transmission, is liveliest at night.
—*Bill Cosby in* Childhood

While nine women insisted that the All-Time Funniest Man they knew was their husband, and another three declared it was their son, a much larger number chose one particular man who's been making us laugh on the small screen, the big screen, on video, on comedy stages, and between the covers of a book, for lo, these many years. A Robin flies not far behind him, a gentle clown appears as a distant third, but it's Bill who pushes our laugh button most consistently.

Here, then, are our Top Ten Funny Fellas:

1. Bill Cosby
2. Robin Williams
3. Red Skelton (Goodnight and God bless you, too, Mr. Skelton)
4. Tim Allen
5. Billy Crystal
6. Tim Conway
7. Jerry Lewis
8. Bob Hope

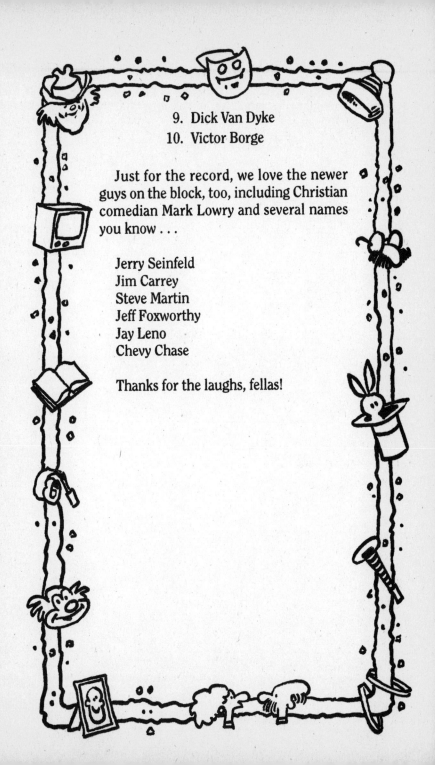

9. Dick Van Dyke
10. Victor Borge

Just for the record, we love the newer guys on the block, too, including Christian comedian Mark Lowry and several names you know . . .

Jerry Seinfeld
Jim Carrey
Steve Martin
Jeff Foxworthy
Jay Leno
Chevy Chase

Thanks for the laughs, fellas!

PART SIX

Humor and Eternity

One Sunday morning Mary's pastor was preaching about heaven, and he said that money wasn't important in the afterlife because in heaven there is no money.

Whereupon her friend Helen whispered to her husband, "You hear that, Bill? We're already in heaven."

There won't be money in heaven, nor marrying, nor tears. But there will be worship and music and praise and joy unspeakable. And, I believe, there will be laughter. It was Martin Luther who said, "If you're not allowed to laugh in heaven, I don't want to go there." Since the many Lutherans among us know their fearless founder will be there, we can surmise that laughter probably will be too.

And grace, Martin. Glorious grace.

CHAPTER 25

Humor and the Lord: Glad Tidings of Great Joy

I have never understood why it should be considered derogatory to the Creator to suppose that he has a sense of humor.
—William Inge

Sandy from Pennsylvania quipped:

He made us in his image,
So he must want us to laugh;
He, no doubt, had a chuckle
When he made the first giraffe!

What makes God laugh? We do, of course! As much as we laugh at our children, knowing so well their personalities, strengths, and weaknesses, why wouldn't God be amused at our antics, even knowing in advance what we're going to say and do? "I just know God has a wonderful sense of humor," insists Mae from Texas. And Karen from Kentucky says, "I firmly believe God has a very strange sense of humor, but then, I've been accused of that myself."

Since God is Spirit and Truth rather than flesh, the laughter might be silent—or it might rock the gates of heaven.

Won't it be fun when we find out?

Some among us already have a sense of what tickles the Lord's funny bone, as it were. Donna from Arkansas writes, "During a very special time in his presence, I sensed God placing a picture of himself in my heart and we laughed together. His eyes were full of love and laughter, and he had a smile so full of joy, I just had to hug him . . . what a moment!" Perhaps she heard what Sir Thomas Browne in 1658 called "that unextinguishable laugh in heaven."

Mary from Michigan affirms, "I'm so glad the Lord laughs at me, with me, in me, and through me," and Donna from Virginia says, "At times when I've done something really ridiculous, I'm sure God is sharing the moment with me."

Sanctified Silliness

Does your church have a sense of humor? Many traditions seem to view humor as the opposite of spirituality. Everything associated with the religious experience is serious, from sermons to orders of service to worship styles. At the other end of the spectrum is the Toronto Blessing, where laughter is part of the revival expression.

How one laughs with the Lord is as individual and private a decision as how one prays, observes communion, or celebrates in worship. My only goal here is to encourage you to consider ways to incorporate more laughter ("expressions of joy," if that sounds more spiritual!) into your daily walk with God.

One church reaches its hand toward the community with a "joy buzzer" hidden in their palm, so to speak. The sign advertising the weekly sermon featured this title: ETERNITY: SMOKING OR NONSMOKING?

Cheryl from Oklahoma spotted this sign on her daughter's office wall: JESUS IS COMING! LOOK BUSY!

Then there was the young woman attending an all-girls Christian school. On her floor of the dorm, they had one rest room that offered four toilets—three with privacy doors and one without. Pat from Utah explains that someone cleverly wrote over each stall: 1 JOHN, 2 JOHN, 3 JOHN, and REVELATION!

Elemental Humor

It's not just the signs of the times that make us laugh in church. It is our own foibles that often tickle us most.

Doris from Texas remembers a recent Christmas Eve service where Communion was served in a special way. Rather than just passing the elements down the pews, the deacons were stationed in the aisles. Participants got up when they were ready and collected their "crackers and grape juice," as Doris calls it.

"I reached in the plate for my cracker and ended up with three stuck together. I returned to my seat with juice and crackers in hand, not knowing that my daughter, Jennifer, had told my husband not to get a cracker because 'Mom had them.'"

Doris popped her three-fold cracker in her mouth, followed by the juice. "It's always a very meaningful time of reflection, made extra special on Christmas Eve. Then I looked at my daughter, who had an expression of horror on her face because I had eaten all the crackers. We got tickled and had to turn away from each other so we wouldn't laugh.

"Meanwhile, my husband has told everyone how I short-changed their Lord's Supper. He said it would've been too embarrassing to get up and get a cracker, since he didr 't want anyone thinking he needed seconds."

Speaking of Communion, I had a hard time not spraying my tiny cup of grape juice all over the pew in front of me one Sunday. I'd invited several of my coworkers to visit my church that particular day because I was singing a solo. It seemed a natural way to share my faith with them and let them be embraced by our warm, loving church fellowship.

One friend from work, Jack, was really made welcome that morning. I was sitting in the front row, preoccupied with getting mentally prepared for my solo, when Jack came in the sanctuary and found a seat at the end of the last pew.

Since our church is so big, with so many new faces, it's hard to know who's been around awhile and who's new or visiting. Apparently the deacons were short a man or two that first service and were desperate for help serving the elements.

Someone leaned down and whispered in Jack's ear, "Could you help us serve Communion?"

"I don't attend here," Jack informed them.

"We don't mind, if you don't. We could really use your help."

In marched Jack with the other deacons, and of course, they started at the first pew. I was busy reviewing the words to my song, oblivious to the Communion crisis going on in the back of the sanctuary, and looked up to see my own guest, Jack, handing me the elements with a huge grin on his face!

Do you suppose the Lord was laughing, too?

Vi from Texas must have had a terrible time keeping a straight face when she accompanied her husband, who was filling in for a much younger pastor one Sunday morning. "As I sat in a pew in the back, an older lady sitting next to me said, 'Honey, are you a visitor?'"

"Yes, I am," Vi assured her.

"Oh, I'm so sorry. We have an old retired preacher filling in today, but you be sure and come back next Sunday. Our pastor will be back, and it will be much better."

Vi has also seen a few hundred baptisms in her time, I'm sure, but the one Dixie is about to describe must have been memorable for all in attendance.

Dixie from Illinois says, "I had never seen a baptism before, and I was so excited. There stood our stern, solemn pastor, waiting at the bottom of the baptistery, not smiling, just waiting for me to descend.

"Bounding down the slippery steps in my excitement, I fell in with a large splash, covering the pastor with water that now dripped from his face. He baptized me—again—still not smiling. Since no one told me to wear white underclothes, I had on my brand-new red bra with panties to match. When I came up out of the water, I wasn't the only one wearing red!"

Pint-Size Humor

Robin thinks, "Some things children do to make you laugh you know are directly from God." Amen, sister, and here's proof

Exhibit #1: Billie from Oklahoma was taking her grandson, Jeff, to Sunday school and gave him a small offering to share. "Here's your money for Jesus," she said.
His eyes opened wide. "Is he gonna be there?"

Exhibit #2: Katrina was tucking her seven-year-old son in bed Easter night and asked him, "What are you thankful for?"
"I'm thankful it's Easter," he declared.
"And what does Easter mean to you?"
"It means Jesus died on the cross for our sins and he was raised again so that we could have *alternative life*."

Exhibit #3: Marian was saying grace and took the opportunity to ask God to grant her five-year-old daughter various qualities that Marian had been suggesting the girl should develop.

When Marian finished, her daughter made a *harrumph!* sound and said, "You weren't praying to God; you were praying at me."

> *Humor is a prelude to faith and laughter is the beginning of prayer.*
>
> —Reinhold Niebuhr

Out of the Mouths of Babes

Renee's mother had only recently come to know Christ as her Savior, and so had much to learn about the Christian faith, about the Bible, and all the myriad facets of her new life in Christ. When her mother came to visit her in Florida, Renee took her to one of the historic churches in the area with a large crucifix. Nailed above it was the sign, written in Greek, Latin, and Hebrew, saying, THIS IS THE KING OF THE JEWS, just as described in Luke 23:38.

"Look, Renee!" her mother exclaimed, pointing at the sign. "In God we trust!"

On another occasion, Renee was discussing various Bible stories with her mother, realizing again how little her mother yet knew about Scripture. Later that day they left for a long car ride, and Renee thought she'd make good use of the time. "So, Mom, what do you know about Adam and Eve?"

Her mother, bless her, looked confused and said, "What were their names? Is that the couple we met yesterday at Walt Disney World?"

Renee could barely get out, "No, Mom, like in the Bible," before her mother caught on. Both laughed hysterically, weaving through traffic with tears streaming down their faces.

We were all babes in the kingdom once. Kinda fun when you're an adult in "spiritual diapers." Humbling yes, but joyful for all.

Does Laughter in the Pulpit Count?

A question I've often posed to the Lord in prayer is simply this: "Is it okay if I'm funny, Lord? In my presentations, in my books, am I truly honoring your name when I cut up and carry on?"

Of course, the humor is clean, never offensive, and that's good. But my query goes deeper than that. I long to know if humor is encouraging and edifying to the body of Christ. Does it count, in terms of glorifying God and building his kingdom? Should I instead be pouring my energy into leading Bible studies and sharing meaningful insights from life and Scripture?

At a Michigan speaking engagement, I was fully prepared to share a strong, meaty message about "Ten Tips for Lifestyle Evangelism." Oh, was it deep stuff. Much note taking would ensue. God will be so proud of me, I thought.

My presentation was on Sunday morning, and there I was at midnight on Saturday, wide awake, stretched across my bed, feeling very uneasy about the next morning. "But, Lord," I said in the direction of the ceiling, "what am I anxious about? This is such a good teaching. A serious Bible study, Lord. Important stuff, right?"

The ceiling wasn't talking, but the Lord was. His still, small voice echoed in my heart. "Liz, think again. Where are your gifts, where is your calling, and what do women respond to most?"

"Oh, yeah," I sighed. "They do like to laugh, and I love to watch it happen. But Lord, does it count? I want to be deep. Deep, like Jill Briscoe or Gloria Gaither or Elisabeth Elliot. Deep, Lord, can't I be deep?"

"You're forgetting the song, Liz: 'Deep and wide. Deep and wide.' You handle the wide part, okay?"

For a minute, I thought I heard him smile.

His words to my heart continued.

"The woman who pours the grape juice into little cups on Saturday night. Is her work deep? Does it honor me?"

"Of course," I assured him.

"The women who sew the costumes for the Easter pageant. Do their labors count deeply for the cause of Christ?"

"Certainly!"

"The man who mows the lawn around the church every Saturday morning. Are his efforts in vain, or do they please my heart?"

I was crying by now. "Okay, okay."

"Put away your Bible study, Liz. I've called others to do that who are, frankly, better at it than you are. But your calling, my child, is to make women laugh with fullness of joy, so that their hearts might be opened to the love and forgiveness I've prepared for them."

"Is that it, Lord?" I sniffed. "It seems so . . . shallow."

Now he reminded me of a Scripture: "Whatever you do, do it heartily, as to the Lord and not to men" (Colossians 3:23).

"Whatever?" I said, then laughed. "I get it, Lord. Laughter comes under the category of whatever!"

Sunday morning dawned with an air of anticipation. I had some wild, scribbled notes and a vague sense of where the message was going, but I'm usually much more organized when I speak. This was scary. "Whatever, Lord," I whispered under my breath. "Hope you enjoy the show."

It seems he did. A dear woman there named Mary slipped me a note: "Thank you for being obedient to God today! The stress in my life has been immense . . . I broke free this weekend through laughter! You were a physician, bringing medication to the afflicted. Psalm 2:4 says, 'He who sits in the heavens shall laugh'!"

Suzi also handed me a note that read, "Even your name begins with *l*—like laughter! You sure do tickle my funny bone and bring me to my knees to face things I need to look at."

Oh, Lord! That's deep!

After that Sunday, my speaking started taking a new turn. I found myself sharing even more humor (without guilt!) at church events, and more of my faith (without fear!) at general events. Kelley heard me at a women's health event sponsored by a hospital in Indiana and wrote me to say, "You truly exhibit the joy, the passion, the adventure of the Christian life!"

Yes! It's wonderful to be walking in the will of the Lord and have it be such a hoot. I'm hardly alone in this. Carol from Alabama says, "I love showing others that it's fun to be a Christian!" Karen thinks "funny Christians witness so much better than sour ones," and Natalie agrees: "If others don't think Christians can have a little fun, they lose interest."

The key is that the humor of one who knows God should be decidedly different from the humor of this world:

Worldly Humor

1. Glorifies sin
2. Puts down others
3. Ridicules righteousness
4. Hurts the spirit

Godly Humor

1. Avoids offense
2. Pokes fun at ourselves
3. Honors the Lord as our source of joy
4. Heals the spirit

Since I believe laughter and music are two of God's finest gifts to his people, I wanted to share this little ditty that I sometimes sing to close my programs.

I wrote it on a plane. (No, not on the side of it! I mean, while flying.) Since I'm an *encourager*, which means in a literal sense, "to fill the heart," and since I love to fill hearts with laughter, it's only fitting that the Lord put this song in my heart for you . . .

Laughter Is the Language of the Heart

Lyrics by Liz Curtis Higgs   *Music by Liz Curtis Higgs*

Laugh - ter   Is the Lan - guage of the Heart.

It   speaks   in a voice   that says

"Come,   let's take part!" It brings joy   to your

soul,   fills you up,   makes you whole;

Laugh-ter,   It's the Lan-guage of the Heart.

Quotable Quotes from Wise Women

Among all the stories you've read here, I've included many of the insightful comments offered by our five hundred contributors as well as quotes from famous people from all walks of life and time.

My favorite statements of all came from "real" women, not famous ones, though they're very well-known by the Father.

> When life becomes too grim, my soul cries out for laughter.
> —Marilyn from Michigan

> Good wholesome laughter is a resurrection of the spirit.
> —Mary Ann from Texas

> Laughter is a gift that we use to displace darkness.
> —Jan from Nevada

It's so true: When your face lights up with laughter, I see Jesus shining through!

About the Author

Liz Curtis Higgs wasn't born funny, but it didn't take long.

The youngest in a family of six children who all saw life through grin-colored glasses, Liz learned at an early age that a sense of humor was like currency—it bought you attention, it bought you applause, it bought you time: "No, you don't have to wash the dishes yet, honey, just tell us another funny story."

When Liz appeared in school plays, they were comedies. In dramas, she played the roles that offered comic relief amid the tragedy. When she wrote for the school paper, her news articles always took a humorous bent.

Liz couldn't help it. Funny stuff just leaked out.

A propensity for humor followed her through ten years as a radio personality, doing every format from jazz to album rock to adult Top-40 to country (for seventeen days). Her second career, in professional speaking, put her on 1,200 platforms in 48 states (Maine and Hawaii, she's ready when you are). Audiences of every stripe have applauded her offbeat, original humor and her heartfelt encouragement.

Liz's first book, published in 1993, brought her humor to the printed page. *"One Size Fits All" and Other Fables* was followed by *Only Angels Can Wing It, the Rest of Us Have to Practice,* then *Forty Reasons Why Life Is More Fun After the Big 4-0* and *Mirror, Mirror on the Wall, Have I Got News for You!*

She's married to Bill Higgs, her favorite source of humorous stories. Together they have two children, Matthew and Lillian, who write comedy material disguised as homework.

For the latest issue of her free newsletter, *The Laughing Heart*®, published twice a year, please write:

Liz Curtis Higgs
P.O. Box 43577
Louisville, KY 40253-0577

GIVE YOURSELF MORE REASONS TO SMILE WITH THESE OTHER GREAT BOOKS FROM LIZ CURTIS HIGGS...

Only Angels Can Wing It

In this humorous look at how to bring balance and grace to a busy life, Liz Curtis Higgs reexamines the many qualities of the "virtuous woman" taking the pressure off today's well-meaning but weary (and less than angelic) wives and mothers. Liz addresses everything from fiscal responsibility to maintaining a happy, comfortable home without burning out...showing women we're doing better than we thought.

0-7852-8247-5 • Trade Paperback • 228 pages

Mirror, Mirror on the Wall, Have I Got News for You!

Liz Curtis Higgs offers an alphabetical journey through God's Word, as she weaves together twin themes that lead to the biblical view of self-worth: Who Christ is in you and Who you are in Christ. In her warm and humorous style, Liz provides memorable stories that will help women discover their timeless beauty and immeasurable worth in the mirror of God's Word.

0-7852-7109-0 • Trade Paperback • 128 pages

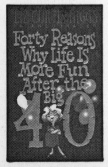

Forty Reasons Why Life Is More Fun After the Big 4-0

Liz Curtis Higgs, along with more than 400 "over 40" women share their often humorous stories of the joys and challenges of life after the age of forty. Liz also shares some hilarious stories of her own fortieth birthday.

0-7852-7615-7 • Trade Paperback • 216 pages